SOUL SLEEP: The Shocking Biblical Truth That Shatters Ghost Myths and Reveals God's Amazing Plan for the Dead

Hard Life Problems Worth Solving

JV SETH

Published by JV SETH, 2026.

SOUL SLEEP: THE SHOCKING BIBLICAL TRUTH THAT SHATTERS GHOST MYTHS AND REVEALS GOD'S AMAZING PLAN FOR THE DEAD

Written by JV SETH.

Table of Contents

SOUL SLEEP:

The Shocking Biblical Truth That Shatters Ghost Myths and Reveals God's Amazing Plan for the Dead

Discover Why the Dead Do Not Haunt Us, What Truly Happens When We Breathe Our Last, and How the True Church of God Holds the Only Key to Eternal Life.

FOREWORD

A Compassionate Invitation to Lay Down the Heavy Burden of Superstitious Fear

Peace be unto you.

From the beginning, the enemy of our souls has used one weapon more effectively than any other to keep humanity in bondage: the fear of the unknown, specifically, the fear of death and what lies beyond it. For generations, we have been taught to dread the dark, to fear the shadows, and to believe that when a loved one takes their final breath, they become a wandering, conscious spirit, capable of haunting the living or suffering in unseen realms. This belief has birthed a heavy, suffocating burden of superstitious fear.

But the Great Teacher, our Lord Jesus Christ, came to shatter the chains of this bondage. He declared, **"You shall know the truth, and the truth shall make you free"** (John 8:32). The Apostle Paul, inspired by the Holy Spirit, echoed this liberating promise: **"For God has not given us a spirit of fear** (phobos - φόβος)**, but of power and of love and of a sound mind"** (2 Timothy 1:7).

This book is not merely a collection of theological arguments; it is a compassionate invitation. It is an invitation to lay down the heavy, terrifying myths of human tradition and embrace the liberating, peaceful truth of God's Word. You will discover that the Creator, in His infinite wisdom and mercy, did not design death to be a terrifying awakening into a ghostly existence. He designed it to be a deep, dreamless, and perfectly peaceful sleep.

As you turn these pages, let your heart be open. Let us reason together, as the Lord invites us in Isaiah 1:18. Let the unadulterated

Word of God wash away the shadows of superstition, replacing them with the brilliant, comforting light of biblical truth. You do not need to fear the dead, for they are safely resting in the hands of the Almighty, awaiting the glorious morning of the resurrection.

Welcome to the truth. Welcome to peace.

PREFACE

From the Terror of Ghost Stories to the Comforting Clarity of Original Biblical Texts

I remember the darkness of my childhood bedroom vividly. Like many, my imagination was captive to the terrifying tales of ghosts, spirits, and the supernatural. Every creak of the floorboards was a phantom; every shadow on the wall was a restless soul. I was taught by well-meaning traditions that when people died, their "souls" floated away, remaining fully conscious, watching over us, or worse, suffering in unseen torment. This belief did not bring comfort; it bred a deep, existential dread.

As I grew older, this dread evolved into a profound intellectual and spiritual crisis. I looked at the world and saw millions paralyzed by the same fear, consulting mediums, fearing curses, and mourning their loved ones with the agonizing belief that they were still consciously suffering or wandering.

Then, I did the most radical, life-changing thing a seeker of truth can do: I stopped listening to human traditions and opened the Bible. I adopted the mindset of a sensible, logical preacher who demands only one thing: **"Ano ang sabi ng Biblia?"** (What does the Bible actually say?). I did not bring my preconceived notions to the text; I let the text speak for itself, diving into the original Hebrew and Greek languages to uncover the unadulterated meaning of the words.

What I found shattered my fears forever.

I discovered that the word "soul" does not mean an immortal ghost. I learned that the Bible never describes the dead as floating, conscious spirits. Instead, I found a God who is so merciful that He calls death a "sleep" (**koimao** - κοιμάω). I found that the dead are not haunting us; they are resting, completely unaware of the world's troubles, safely preserved in the memory of the Creator until the day He calls them forth.

This book is the culmination of that journey. It is written for the 12-year-old who is afraid of the dark, and for the adult who is grieving the loss of a parent. It is written with the razor-sharp logic of a scholar and the tender, compassionate heart of a shepherd. My prayer is that as you read, the terror of ghost stories will vanish, replaced by the profound, unshakable comfort of original biblical truth.

INTRODUCTION

The Great Deception and the Great Comfort

We live in an age obsessed with the supernatural. Turn on a television, scroll through social media, or walk into a bookstore, and you will be inundated with stories of ghosts, near-death experiences, and communication with the dead. Humanity is gripped by a deep, existential dread, desperately searching for meaning and connection beyond the grave. Yet, in this frantic search, we have forgotten what the Creator originally designed. We have allowed human philosophy and ancient pagan myths to overwrite the clear, plain teachings of the Holy Scriptures.

It is time to pull back the curtain. It is time to expose the Great Deception and embrace the Great Comfort.

The Great Deception is the lie that human beings possess an immortal, detachable "soul" that floats away as a conscious ghost upon death. This idea did not originate in the Bible; it originated in ancient Greek philosophy, notably from thinkers like Plato, and was later woven into religious traditions. But we are not governed by Greek philosophy; we are governed by the Word of God.

Let us apply clear, critical thinking and look at the very first mention of the "soul" in the Bible. In **Genesis 2:7**, we read: **"And the Lord God formed man of the dust of the ground, and breathed into his nostrils the breath of life; and man became a living soul."**

Notice the phrasing carefully. The Bible does not say God put a soul **into** the man. It says man **became** a living soul. In the original Hebrew, the word used is **Nephesh** (נֶפֶשׁ), which simply means a breathing creature, a life, or a being. When combined with **Chayyah**

(חַיָּה), meaning "living," the phrase **Nephesh Chayyah** (נֶפֶשׁ חַיָּה) means a "living being."

Think of it like a lamp. The clay and glass are the body (the dust). The electricity is the breath of life (the **Ruach** - רוּחַ, or spirit/breath). When you combine the lamp and the electricity, you get light. The light is not a separate entity that floats away when the lamp is turned off; the light **is** the lamp functioning. In the same way, you do not **have** a soul; you **are** a soul. Your body plus the breath of life from God equals a living soul.

Therefore, what happens when the electricity is turned off? The light does not float around the room as a "ghost of light." The light simply ceases to exist until the power is turned back on.

This brings us to the Great Comfort. The Bible is remarkably consistent on the state of the dead. King Solomon, granted unparalleled wisdom by God, wrote in **Ecclesiastes 9:5**: **"For the living know that they will die, but the dead know nothing."** The Hebrew word for "nothing" here is absolute. It means no consciousness, no memory, no pain, no haunting, and no awareness of time.

When a person dies, the body returns to the dust, and the **Ruach** (רוּחַ - breath of life) returns to God who gave it (Ecclesiastes 12:7). The person enters a state the Bible consistently calls "sleep." In the New Testament, the Greek word used is **Koimao** (κοιμάω), from which we get the word "cemetery" (koimeterion, a sleeping place). Jesus Himself used this exact term when His friend Lazarus died. He did not say, "Lazarus's soul is in heaven looking down on us." He said, **"Our friend Lazarus has fallen asleep, but I go that I may wake him up"** (John 11:11).

If the dead are merely sleeping, unconscious and at peace, then the terrifying tales of ghosts, hauntings, and conscious torment in an underworld are not just false; they are a dangerous deception. The Apostle Paul warns us that in the latter times, some will depart from the faith, **"giving heed to deceiving spirits and doctrines of demons"**

(1 Timothy 4:1). Any "spirit" that claims to be a deceased loved one is, by biblical definition, a counterfeit, for the dead are asleep and cannot speak (Psalm 115:17).

This book is your guide out of the darkness of superstition and into the marvelous light of biblical truth. We will journey through the original Hebrew and Greek texts, applying logic, critical thinking, and unwavering faith in the Scriptures alone. We will answer the unspoken questions of our age: **Where are my loved ones? Are they in pain? Can they hear me?**

The answer, beautifully and mercifully, is this: They are not in pain. They are not wandering. They are resting in the loving, protective sleep of the Lord, safely preserved in His memory, awaiting the glorious, triumphant day when the trumpet shall sound, the dead shall be raised incorruptible, and we shall be changed (1 Corinthians 15:52).

Let us turn the page, open our Bibles, and let the truth set us free.

PART I: THE ANATOMY OF A LIVING SOUL

(Universal Themes of Identity & Meaning; Intellectual Depth through Original Languages)

Chapter 1: You Are Not a Ghost in a Machine

- **Description:** Dismantles the Greek philosophical idea of an immortal, detachable soul. Explores **Genesis 2:7**, revealing that God did not **put** a soul into a body; rather, the combination of dust and the breath of life (**neshamah**) made man a **living soul** (**nephesh chayyah** - נֶפֶשׁ חַיָּה). You do not **have** a soul; you **are** a soul.

Imagine, for a moment, a beautiful, handcrafted clay lamp. By itself, sitting on a table, it is merely shaped earth. It has no light. It has no warmth. It is just clay. Now, imagine running an electrical current through it. Suddenly, the lamp glows. It illuminates the room.

If you unplug the lamp, does the "light" float around the room as a conscious, glowing ghost, searching for a new socket? Of course not. The light was not a separate entity trapped inside the clay. The light was the **result** of the clay and the electricity working together. When the power is removed, the light simply ceases to exist until the power is restored.

For centuries, humanity has been taught a very different, deeply confusing story about ourselves. We have been told that we are merely "ghosts driving a meat-covered skeleton," as the popular saying goes. We have been led to believe that our physical bodies are temporary, decaying cages, and that inside each of us resides an immortal, detachable "soul" that will float away the moment our hearts stop beating.

But we must ask the most critical, sensible question a seeker of truth can ask: **"Ano ang sabi ng Biblia?"** (What does the Bible actually say?)

We must not lean on ancient Greek philosophy, which heavily promoted the idea of an immortal, detachable soul. We must not rely on human traditions or spooky campfire tales. We must go to the very foundation of truth: the unadulterated, original text of the Holy Scriptures.

Let us turn to the very first mention of the "soul" in the entire Bible.

"And the Lord God formed man of the dust of the ground, and breathed into his nostrils the breath of life; and man became a living soul." (Genesis 2:7, KJV)

Let us examine this verse with the precision of a scholar and the clarity of a teacher. In the original Hebrew text, this verse is a masterclass in divine engineering. It contains three specific elements:

1. **The Dust:** The Hebrew word used here is **Aphar** (עָפָר), which means dust, earth, or dry soil. This represents the physical, tangible body.

2. **The Breath:** The Hebrew word is **Neshamah** (נְשָׁמָה), meaning breath, or the animating breath of life. This is the divine spark, the energy given by the Creator.

3. **The Result:** The Hebrew phrase is **Nephesh Chayyah** (נֶפֶשׁ חַיָּה), which translates to "living soul" or "living being."

Notice the verb carefully. The Bible does **not** say that God put a soul **into** the man. It says that man **became** a living soul. The Hebrew verb used is **Hayah** (הָיָה), which means "to become" or "to be."

This is a monumental distinction. It means that the soul is not something you **have**; it is something you **are**.

Think of it as a divine equation:

Dust (Aphar) + Breath of Life (Neshamah) = Living Soul (Nephesh Chayyah)

You are the sum of these parts. You are a unified, magnificent creation. You are not a ghost haunting a machine. You are a living, breathing being, intricately woven by the hands of God.

Now, let us apply clear, critical thinking to this truth. If the "soul" is an immortal, conscious ghost that floats away at death, we must ask: Does this definition hold up throughout the rest of the Bible?

The answer is a resounding no. The Hebrew word **Nephesh** (נֶפֶשׁ) is used over 700 times in the Old Testament, and it simply means a "living, breathing creature." It is not exclusive to humans.

Look at what God created on the fifth day:

"And God said, Let the waters bring forth abundantly the moving creature that hath life [nephesh]**..."** (Genesis 1:20)

"And God created great whales, and every living creature [nephesh chayyah] that moveth..." (Genesis 1:21)

If a "soul" is an immortal, thinking, feeling ghost that survives death, then we are forced into a logical absurdity: Do fish have immortal, thinking ghosts? Do cattle and birds possess eternal, conscious spirits that float to a heavenly pasture when they die?

Logic and Scripture demand a consistent definition. The Bible is clear: humans, animals, and birds are all described as **Nephesh**. They are all living, breathing beings. The difference between humanity and the animals is not that we have a "soul" and they do not; the difference is that humanity was uniquely formed from the dust and given the direct breath of life (**Neshamah**) by God, making us accountable, moral beings created in His image.

Why does this matter? Why is this truth so profoundly important for a twelve-year-old reading this in their bedroom, or an adult grieving in a hospital waiting room?

Because this truth dismantles fear.

If you believe you are a detachable ghost, you will live in fear of death, fearing that your conscious spirit will be ripped from your body to wander in darkness or suffer in torment. You will fear the creaking floorboards, the shadows in the hall, and the supposed "spirits" of the departed.

But when you understand the biblical truth, a magnificent peace washes over you. You realize that your body is not a prison. It is the sacred clay molded by the Creator. Your life is a precious, unified gift. And when that life ends, the Bible does not describe a terrifying extraction of a conscious ghost. It describes the gentle turning off of the lamp. The breath (**Neshamah**) returns to God who gave it (Ecclesiastes 12:7), the body returns to the dust (**Aphar**), and the living soul (**Nephesh**) ceases its earthly activity, entering a state of peaceful, dreamless sleep, safely preserved in the memory of the Almighty until the day of resurrection.

You are not a temporary prisoner in a decaying shell. You are a masterpiece of dust and divine breath. You are a living soul.

And because you are a living soul, created by a God who holds the keys of life and death, you have nothing to fear from the shadows. The truth has set you free.

As we turn the page, we will explore the very breath that animates this clay, and discover what the Bible truly means when it says the "spirit" returns to God.

Chapter 2: The Breath of the Almighty

- **Description:** A profound study of the Hebrew word **Ruach** (רוּחַ) and Greek **Pneuma** (πνεῦμα). Explains that the "spirit" that returns to God at death (Ecclesiastes 12:7) is not a conscious, floating personality, but the very breath of life and the animating power given by the Creator, much like electricity returning to the grid when a lamp is turned off.

Beloved, let us reason together.

When a loved one takes their final breath, a profound and universal question echoes in the human heart: **Where did they go?** Our culture, saturated with tales of near-death experiences and wandering spirits, eagerly whispers a comforting but dangerous lie: "Their spirit is still here. Their conscious soul is floating nearby, watching over you."

But we must not be swept away by the emotional currents of human tradition. We must anchor our minds to the bedrock of divine truth. We must ask the most sensible, critical question a seeker of truth can ask: **"Ano ang sabi ng Biblia?"** (What does the Bible actually say?)

To understand what happens at the moment of death, we must understand the very essence of what keeps us alive. We must examine the original languages of the Scriptures, for God's Word is a precise, flawless instrument.

In the Old Testament, the Hebrew word most commonly translated as "spirit" is **Ruach** (רוּחַ).

In the New Testament, the Greek equivalent is **Pneuma** (πνεῦμα).

What do these words actually mean in their original, unadulterated context? They do not primarily mean a "ghost" or a "disembodied personality." In both Hebrew and Greek, these words fundamentally mean **wind, breath, or animating power**.

Let us look at the evidence, clearly and thoroughly, so that both a young student and a seasoned scholar can grasp this magnificent truth.

In **Genesis 7:22**, describing the flood, the Bible states: **"All in whose nostrils was the breath of the spirit of life** (nishmat ruach chayim - **נִשְׁמַת רוּחַ חַיִּים**)**, all that was in the dry land, died."**

Notice the pairing. The "spirit" (**Ruach**) is directly linked to the "breath" (**Nishmat**) in the nostrils. It is the physical, animating breath of life that God breathes into the clay.

King David, inspired by the Holy Spirit, beautifully captures this dependency in **Psalm 104:29**: **"You hide Your face, they are troubled; You take away their breath** (Ruach)**, they die and return to their dust."**

When God withdraws the **Ruach**, the person does not become a floating, conscious ghost. The Bible is explicit: they **die** and return to dust. The animating power is removed.

The Apostle James, writing in the New Testament, confirms this exact same principle using the Greek word **Pneuma** (πνεῦμα). In **James 2:26**, he writes: **"For as the body without the spirit** (pneuma) **is dead, so faith without works is dead also."**

Just as a car without an engine is merely a shell, a human body without the **Pneuma**—the breath of life—is a corpse. It is not a "haunted" body; it is a lifeless body.

Now, we arrive at the masterpiece verse that has been misunderstood for centuries. Let us read it with fresh, critical eyes:

"Then the dust will return to the earth as it was, and the spirit (Ruach - **רוּחַ**) **will return to God who gave it."** (Ecclesiastes 12:7)

Traditional theology looks at this verse and imagines a conscious, chattering personality floating up to heaven the moment the heart stops. But let us apply clear, logical thinking.

If the **Ruach** is the conscious personality, then at this very moment, God is hosting billions of conscious, talking, earth-aware personalities floating in His presence. But we have already established from **Ecclesiastes 9:5** that "the dead know nothing." They do not have conscious thoughts, memories, or awareness.

Therefore, logic and Scripture demand a harmonious conclusion: The **Ruach** that returns to God is **not the conscious personality**. It is the **animating life force**, the breath of life, the divine energy that God lent to us.

To make this profoundly clear, let us use an analogy that a twelve-year-old can easily understand, yet holds deep intellectual weight for an adult.

Imagine a beautiful, intricately designed lamp sitting in a dark room. The lamp represents your physical body, formed from the dust of the earth. Now, imagine plugging that lamp into a massive, powerful electrical grid. The electricity represents the **Ruach** (רוּחַ), the breath of life from God.

When the electricity flows through the lamp, it produces light. The light is beautiful, warm, and alive. But here is the critical question: If you unplug the lamp, does the "light" detach itself and float around the room as a conscious "ghost of light," looking for a new socket?

Of course not. That is absurd.

When the lamp is unplugged, the electricity simply ceases to animate the bulb. The light goes out. The power returns to the grid, and the lamp returns to being just a lamp. The "light" was not a separate entity; it was the **result** of the lamp and the electricity working together.

This is the exact biblical model of human life.

Body (Dust) + Ruach (Breath of Life from God) = Living Soul (You).

When death occurs, it is not a terrifying extraction of a conscious ghost. It is the divine "unplugging." The body returns to the dust. The **Ruach**—the animating breath of life—returns to God, the great Power Grid of the universe, who gave it. The conscious "you" ceases to exist in this world, entering a state of peaceful, dreamless sleep, safely preserved in the perfect memory of the Creator.

Why is this truth so emotionally resonant and deeply comforting?

Because it destroys the nightmare of spiritualism. If you believe your loved one's "spirit" is still consciously floating around, you will live in anxiety. You will wonder if they are cold, if they are in pain, or if they are trying to send you confusing, terrifying "signs." You will be vulnerable to the deceiving spirits and mediums that the Bible strictly forbids (Deuteronomy 18:10-12).

But when you understand that the **Ruach** is the breath of the Almighty, a profound peace washes over your soul. Your loved one is not wandering. They are not suffering. They are not trapped in a ghostly limbo. They are resting. The breath of life that animated them has been safely returned to the loving hands of the Father, who will hold it securely until the glorious day of the resurrection, when He will breathe life into the dust once more.

You are not a ghost trapped in a machine of flesh. You are a magnificent, unified creation, animated by the very breath of the Almighty. And because your life is a precious, borrowed gift from the Creator, it is entirely in His safekeeping.

As we turn the page, we will confront the most dangerous myth of traditional theology head-on. We will prove, using the Bible's own words, that the soul is not immortal, and that the promise of eternal life is not something you are born with, but something you must receive.

Chapter 3: The Mortal Soul: What the Bible Actually Says

- **Description:** Confronts the most dangerous myth of traditional theology. Uses **Ezekiel 18:4** and **18:20** ("The soul who sins shall die") and **Revelation 16:3** (where every living **psyche** in the sea died) to prove biblically that the soul is mortal. If the soul were inherently immortal, it could not die. God alone possesses immortality (1 Timothy 6:16).

My beloved child, let us now confront the most dangerous, deeply entrenched myth in all of human religious history. It is a doctrine that has caused more fear, more despair, and more distortion of God's character than perhaps any other. It is the myth of the "immortal soul."

For centuries, we have been told a story that sounds poetic but is entirely foreign to the Scriptures: the idea that every human being is born with an indestructible, eternal spirit that can never cease to exist. According to this tradition, when the body dies, this immortal soul simply changes addresses, floating off to either eternal bliss or eternal, conscious torment.

But we must not be passive recipients of human tradition. We must be like the noble Bereans, searching the Scriptures daily to see if these things are so (Acts 17:11). We must apply clear, critical thinking and ask the most sensible, piercing question a truth-seeker can ask: **"Ano ang talagang sinasabi ng Biblia?"** (What does the Bible **actually** say?)

Let us put the myth of the immortal soul to the test of divine logic.

The definition of "immortal" is simple: it means **unable to die.** It is a logical impossibility for something to be truly immortal and yet experience death. If the soul is inherently immortal, it cannot die. Period.

Now, let us open the unadulterated Word of God and see if the Bible supports this claim.

The Prophet Ezekiel, speaking the very words of the Almighty, delivers a devastating blow to the myth of the immortal soul. Listen carefully to the clarity of **Ezekiel 18:4**:

"Behold, all souls are Mine; the soul of the father as well as the soul of the son is Mine; the soul who sins shall die."

Let us examine the original Hebrew. The word translated as "soul" here is **Nephesh** (נֶפֶשׁ), which, as we established, means a living, breathing being. The word translated as "die" is **Mut** (מוּת). In Hebrew, **Mut** does not mean "to move to another dimension." It does not mean "to live on in a spiritual realm." It means to perish, to cease living, to come to an absolute end.

God Himself declares through His prophet: **The Nephesh that sins, it shall Mut.** The soul that sins shall die.

Ezekiel repeats this exact same warning in verse 20: **"The soul who sins shall die."** If the soul were inherently immortal, God would be speaking a logical contradiction. But God cannot lie (Titus 1:2). Therefore, the only logical, biblical conclusion is that the soul is **mortal.** It is subject to death.

Perhaps you might think, "Well, that is just the Old Testament. The New Testament must teach that the soul is immortal." Let us turn to the very last book of the Bible, the Book of Revelation, and apply the same rigorous scrutiny.

In **Revelation 16:3**, the Apostle John records a vision of the end times:

"Then the second angel poured out his bowl on the sea, and it became blood as of a dead man; and every living soul died in the sea."

Let us look at the original Greek text. The word used here for "soul" is **Psyche** (ψυχή). The verse explicitly states that every living **psyche** in the sea **died**.

Pause and think about this with me. If the **psyche** (soul) is an immortal, indestructible ghost, how is it possible for it to die in the sea? Can an immortal thing die? No. But if the **psyche** is the living, breathing creature—the fish, the marine life, the unified being—then it makes perfect, logical sense. When the sea turns to blood, the living creatures in it perish. Their souls die.

The Bible is remarkably consistent. From Genesis to Revelation, the soul is not an immortal entity; it is a mortal, living being that is entirely dependent on God for its continued existence.

This brings us to the supreme, undeniable authority on the subject of immortality. The Apostle Paul, inspired by the Holy Spirit, settles this debate once and for all in his first letter to Timothy. He is describing the majestic, awe-inspiring nature of God, and in **1 Timothy 6:15-16**, he writes:

"...He who is the blessed and only Potentate, the King of kings and Lord of lords, who alone has immortality (athanasia - **ἀθανασία), dwelling in unapproachable light..."**

Read that again. God **alone** has immortality.

The Greek word used here is **Athanasia** (ἀθανασία), which literally means "deathlessness." Paul does not say God **primarily** has immortality, or that He shares it inherently with all humans at birth. He says God **alone** possesses it.

If human beings were born with immortal souls, Paul's statement would be a blatant falsehood. But Paul is telling the absolute truth.

Humans are mortal. We are dust. We are entirely dependent on the Creator for every breath we take. Immortality is not our birthright; it is a divine gift that must be sought and received. As Paul writes in **Romans 2:7**, eternal life is for those who **"by patient continuance in doing good seek for glory, honor, and immortality."** You cannot seek something you already inherently possess.

Let us make this profoundly clear with an analogy that a twelve-year-old can easily grasp, yet holds deep intellectual weight for the wisest scholar.

Imagine a candle burning brightly in a dark room. The wax and the wick represent the physical body. The heat and oxygen represent the breath of life (**Ruach**) from God. Together, they produce a beautiful, dancing flame. That flame is the "soul"—the living, active presence of the candle.

Now, imagine someone blowing out the candle. What happens to the flame? Does it detach itself and float up to "flame heaven," consciously watching the room? Does it go to a place of "eternal flame torment" under the floorboards?

Of course not. That is absurd.

When the candle is blown out, the flame simply ceases to exist. The conditions that created the flame are no longer present. The flame is not "immortal." It is entirely dependent on the wax, the wick, and the air. When those are removed, the flame dies.

This is the beautiful, logical, and biblical reality of human life. You are the flame of life, kindled by the breath of the Almighty. When death comes, the flame does not become a ghost. It ceases. The soul dies.

Now, you might ask, **"Why is this good news? Doesn't this make death terrifying?"**

On the contrary, my beloved. This is the most liberating, emotionally resonant truth you will ever discover.

Think about the alternative. If the traditional myth were true, it would mean that God created billions of human beings with an inescapable, indestructible soul, fully aware that many of them would end up suffering in conscious, eternal torment forever. It would make God a cosmic torturer, and it would make human existence a terrifying trap.

But the biblical truth reveals a God of profound mercy and justice. Because the soul is mortal, death is not a gateway to eternal conscious torment; it is a merciful cessation of suffering. It is a deep, dreamless sleep. The wicked do not burn forever; they are consumed and perish, which the Bible calls the "second death" (Revelation 21:8).

Furthermore, this truth magnifies the breathtaking sacrifice of Jesus Christ. If we were already immortal, why did Jesus have to die on the cross? Why did He say, **"I came that they may have life, and that they may have it more abundantly"** (John 10:10)? He came to give us the very thing we do not naturally possess: immortality. Through His resurrection, He conquered death, offering the free gift of eternal life to all who believe in Him (Romans 6:23).

You are not an immortal ghost trapped in a dying body. You are a mortal, magnificent creation, entirely dependent on the grace of God. And because your life is a fragile, precious gift, it is infinitely valuable to the One who gave it.

Do not fear the myth of the immortal soul. Embrace the biblical truth of the mortal soul, for it is this very truth that makes the promise of the resurrection so gloriously necessary, and the grace of God so profoundly beautiful.

As we turn the page, we will step into the profound silence of the grave, and discover the deep, comforting peace of what the Bible truly calls "The Great Slumber."

PART II: THE GREAT SILENCE

(Emotional Resonance for the Grieving; Aesthetic Beauty in describing God's peace)

Chapter 4: The Unconscious Slumber

- **Description:** A deeply comforting chapter for those who have lost loved ones. Explores **Ecclesiastes 9:5-6** and **Psalm 146:4**. When the breath departs, thoughts perish. The dead do not know anything, they do not feel pain, and they do not watch over us from the clouds. They are at absolute, perfect rest, free from the struggles of this world.

My beloved child, if you have ever stood by a graveside, held the hand of a fading loved one, or stared at an empty chair at the dinner table, you know the profound ache of separation. In those moments of deep grief, the human heart desperately searches for comfort. We want to believe that our loved ones are still near, that they are watching over us, guiding us, or at least aware of our tears.

It is a beautiful sentiment, often repeated in sympathy cards and well-meaning traditions: **"They are in a better place, looking down on you right now."**

But we must pause. We must apply clear, compassionate, and critical thinking. Because while that idea might sound comforting at first glance, it actually plants a seed of deep, hidden anxiety in the grieving heart. If our loved ones are consciously watching us from the clouds, do they see our struggles and feel helpless? Do they witness our mistakes and feel disappointment? Are they aware of the pain of this world, unable to intervene?

The Great Teacher, who wept at the tomb of His friend Lazarus, does not leave us to guess or to lean on fragile human traditions. He offers us a comfort that is far deeper, far more logical, and far more peaceful than the myth of the watching ghost.

Let us ask the most sensible, grounding question: **"Ano ang sabi ng Biblia?"** (What does the Bible actually say about the consciousness of the dead?)

The answer is found in the profound, poetic, and absolute wisdom of King Solomon, who was granted unparalleled understanding by God. In **Ecclesiastes 9:5-6**, the Scripture declares:

"For the living know that they will die; but the dead know nothing, and they have no more reward, for the memory of them is forgotten. Also their love, their hatred, and their envy have now perished; nevermore will they have a share in anything done under the sun."

Let us examine this with the precision of a scholar. The Hebrew word used for "know" here is **Yada** (יָדַע). It does not mean a vague, partial awareness. It means comprehensive knowledge, perception, and consciousness. Solomon states plainly: the dead **Yada** nothing. Zero.

Furthermore, the verse states that their love, hatred, and envy have **perished**. The Hebrew word for perished is **Abad** (אָבַד), which means to vanish, to cease, to be lost. When a person dies, the emotional turmoil, the physical pain, the anxieties, and the struggles of this world instantly vanish. They are no longer participants in the "toil under the sun." They are completely, utterly free from the burdens of earthly life.

The Psalmist David echoes this absolute truth in **Psalm 146:4**:

"His spirit departs, he returns to his earth; in that very day his plans perish."

Let us look at the original Hebrew. When a person's **Ruach** (רוּחַ - breath of life) departs and they return to the earth, their **Machshebah**

(מַחֲשָׁבָה - thoughts, plans, or intentions) **Abad** (אָבַד - perish) on that very same day.

Think about the profound clarity of this. The moment the breath leaves the body, the thoughts cease. There is no lingering consciousness. There is no floating, disembodied mind pondering its next move.

To understand this clearly, whether you are twelve years old or eighty, consider a modern analogy. Imagine a brilliant, complex computer running a sophisticated program. The hardware is the body (the dust). The electricity is the **Ruach** (the breath of life). The program running on the screen is the **Machshebah** (the thoughts and consciousness).

What happens the exact millisecond the power cord is pulled from the wall? Does the computer continue to think? Does the screen remain glowing with a "ghost" of the program? Does it feel the absence of power?

No. The screen goes instantly black. The thoughts perish. The machine is at rest. It does not suffer. It does not worry. It simply waits, in absolute silence, for the Creator to plug it in again.

This is the biblical reality of death. It is not a haunting. It is not a state of conscious waiting. It is an **unconscious slumber**.

Some might recoil from this, thinking, **"But that sounds so sad! They are just gone!"**

On the contrary, my beloved. This is the most merciful, emotionally resonant truth you can ever embrace.

If the traditional myth were true, death would be a continuation of earthly anxiety. The dead would be conscious of the decaying of their bodies, conscious of the grief of their families, yet utterly powerless to comfort them. That is not the design of a loving Creator.

But the biblical truth reveals a God of profound tenderness. When the struggles of life become too heavy, when the body grows weary and the heart is broken, God does not condemn the soul to an eternity of conscious, helpless observation. Instead, He gently closes the book. He turns off the light. He grants the ultimate, dreamless, painless sleep.

Your loved one is not watching you cry. They are not feeling the cold of the grave. They are not suffering in a fiery underworld or wandering as a confused spirit. They are at absolute, perfect rest. Their pain has ended. Their worries have ceased. They are safely preserved in the flawless, infinite memory of the Almighty, waiting for the day when the Great Physician will wake them from their slumber.

This truth provides immense practical value for how we live and grieve today. It frees us from the superstitious fear of "signs" or "hauntings." When you hear a floorboard creak or feel a sudden chill, you do not need to fear that it is a restless spirit. The dead are asleep. They cannot disturb you, and you cannot disturb them.

Instead, this truth directs our focus exactly where it belongs: not to the silent grave, but to the living God who holds the power of resurrection. We do not talk to the dead, for they cannot hear us. We talk to the God of the living, thanking Him for the time we had with our loved ones, and trusting Him with their peaceful rest.

The grave is not a theater of conscious torment or ghostly wandering. It is a sanctuary of divine silence. And in that silence, there is profound peace.

As we turn the page, we will explore how even the Master Teacher, our Lord Jesus Christ, consistently used this very language of "sleep" to describe death, reinforcing this beautiful, unshakable hope.

Chapter 5: The Grave Has No Voice

- **Description:** Examines **Psalm 115:17** ("The dead do not praise the LORD") and **Isaiah 38:18**. Explores the biblical concept of **Sheol** (שְׁאוֹל) and **Hades** (ᾅδης) not as a place of conscious torment or ghostly wandering, but simply as the "grave" or the "state of death." The dead are silent, awaiting the Master's call.

My beloved child, let us reason together.

In moments of profound grief, the human heart cries out for a sound. We stand in the quiet aftermath of loss and desperately wish to hear a familiar voice, to receive a sign, or to feel a comforting whisper from beyond the veil. Our culture eagerly feeds this longing. We are surrounded by stories of mediums, psychic readings, and modern "grief-tech" that promises to simulate the voices of the departed.

But we must pause. We must apply clear, critical, and compassionate thinking. We must not allow our deep emotional longing to blind us to the absolute truth of the Creator's design. We must ask the most sensible, grounding question a truth-seeker can ask: **"Ano ang sabi ng Biblia?"** (What does the Bible actually say?)

When we turn to the unadulterated Word of God, we discover a truth that is both profoundly sobering and deeply, beautifully comforting: **The grave has no voice.**

Let us examine the divine testimony. King David, a man after God's own heart, wrote with absolute clarity in **Psalm 115:17**:

"The dead do not praise the LORD, nor any who go down into silence."

Let us look at the original Hebrew text. The word translated as "silence" here is **Dumah** (דּוּמָה). It does not mean a quiet room where people are whispering. It means absolute stillness, a state of being completely hushed, devoid of activity, thought, or sound. The dead do not go to a bustling spiritual realm; they go down into **Dumah**. They enter a state of perfect, unbroken silence.

The Prophet Isaiah reinforces this magnificent truth. When King Hezekiah was healed from a mortal illness, he composed a song of gratitude to God. In **Isaiah 38:18**, he declares:

"For Sheol cannot thank You, death cannot praise You; those who go down into the pit cannot hope for Your truth."

Here, we encounter one of the most misunderstood words in all of religious history: **Sheol** (שְׁאוֹל).

For centuries, human tradition and pagan mythology have painted **Sheol** as a terrifying, fiery underworld—a place of conscious torment, wailing, and ghostly wandering. But we must strip away the myths and look at the biblical definition.

In the original Hebrew, **Sheol** (שְׁאוֹל) simply means "the grave," "the pit," or "the state of death." It is the common destination of all humanity, regardless of their moral standing in life. It is not a place of punishment; it is a place of waiting. It is the great, silent dormitory of the earth.

If **Sheol** were a place of conscious torment or ghostly activity, then the dead **could** thank God, or at least complain about their condition.

But Isaiah states plainly: **Sheol** cannot thank You. Death cannot praise You. Why? Because the dead are not conscious. They are asleep.

Now, let us apply our critical thinking to the New Testament. When the apostles wrote in Greek, how did they translate the Hebrew concept of **Sheol**? They used the Greek word **Hades** (ᾅδης).

Just like **Sheol**, the biblical use of **Hades** (ᾅδης) does not refer to the mythological Greek underworld of torture. In the Scriptures, it strictly means the grave or the state of death.

Listen to the Apostle Peter, quoting King David in **Acts 2:27** (and repeating it in Acts 2:31):

"For You will not leave my soul in Hades, nor will You allow Your Holy One to see corruption."

Peter is not saying that Jesus' conscious spirit went to a place of torment or a waiting room of ghosts. He is declaring that God would not leave the Messiah's body to decay in the **grave** (Hades). The grave could not hold Him. He slept in the dust, and on the third day, the power of God awakened Him to incorruptible life.

To make this profoundly clear, let us use an analogy that a twelve-year-old can easily grasp, yet holds deep intellectual weight for the wisest scholar.

Imagine a magnificent, endless library. In this library, every human being who has ever lived is represented by a beautifully written book. While a person is alive, their book is open. The pages are turning, the story is unfolding, and the words are being read. This is life.

But what happens when a person dies? The Great Librarian gently closes the book. He places it on a shelf in the archives.

Now, ask yourself: Does the closed book read itself in the dark? Does it complain about the silence? Does it float off the shelf to haunt the library?

Of course not. That is absurd.

The closed book is simply waiting. It is in a state of perfect preservation. It holds no consciousness, no pain, and no awareness of time. It simply rests on the shelf, safely kept by the Librarian, awaiting the day He decides to open it once more.

This is the biblical reality of **Sheol** and **Hades**. The grave is not a theater of conscious suffering or ghostly wandering. It is the silent archive of God.

Why is this truth so emotionally resonant and practically valuable for us today?

First, it destroys the dangerous deception of spiritualism. The Bible strictly forbids consulting the dead (Deuteronomy 18:10-12). Why would a loving God forbid something so harmless if the dead could actually talk to us? He forbids it precisely **because** the dead are silent. Therefore, any "voice" claiming to be a deceased loved one is, by biblical definition, a counterfeit. It is a deceiving spirit masquerading as light (2 Corinthians 11:14). Knowing that the grave has no voice protects you from the terrifying and manipulative traps of the occult.

Second, it brings profound peace to the grieving heart. You do not need to worry that your departed loved one is cold, lonely, or consciously suffering in a fiery pit. They are not. They are in **Dumah** (דּוּמָה)—perfect, painless silence. Their struggles are over. Their tears have been wiped away by the very act of sleep.

The silence of the grave is not a tragedy; it is a divine safeguard. It is the quiet, peaceful pause before the glorious symphony of the resurrection.

The dead do not praise the Lord **now**, because they are resting. But the promise of the Bible is that a day is coming when the silence will be broken. Not by the wails of the tormented, but by the triumphant, life-giving voice of the Son of God, calling His beloved ones forth from the archives of the earth to live forever.

Until that glorious morning, the grave has no voice. And in that holy silence, there is perfect peace.

As we turn the page, we will discover how the Master Teacher Himself, our Lord Jesus Christ, consistently used this very language of "sleep" to describe death, cementing this beautiful, unshakable hope as the foundation of our faith.

Chapter 6: Jesus Called It "Sleep"

- **Description:** Highlights the Master's own terminology. In **John 11:11-14**, Jesus does not say Lazarus's soul went to heaven or hell; He says, "Our friend Lazarus has fallen asleep." Explores the New Testament Greek word **koimao** (κοιμάω), used consistently by the apostles (Acts 7:60, 1 Corinthians 15:6, 1 Thessalonians 4:13) to describe death as a peaceful, temporary slumber.

My beloved child, let us reason together.

When the shadow of death falls upon a home, the immediate, desperate question of the human heart is always the same: **"Where are they now?"** Our culture, desperate for comfort, has invented a thousand poetic answers. We are told they have "passed on," that their soul has "flown to a better place," or that they are "looking down on us from heaven."

But we must not be swept away by the emotional currents of well-meaning traditions. We must anchor our minds to the bedrock of divine truth. We must ask the most sensible, piercing question a seeker of truth can ask: **"Ano ang sabi ng Biblia?"** (What does the Bible actually say?)

To find the ultimate authority on this matter, we must go directly to the Master Teacher, our Lord Jesus Christ. He is the Resurrection and the Life. He holds the keys of death and Hades. How did He describe the passing of His dear friend?

Let us turn to the Gospel of John, chapter 11. Lazarus, a man Jesus loved deeply, had fallen gravely ill. His sisters, Mary and Martha, sent an urgent message to Jesus: **"Lord, behold, he whom You love is sick"** (John 11:3).

Notice what Jesus said in response. He did not say, "Lazarus's soul will soon be with Me in heaven." He did not say, "Do not worry, his conscious spirit will be watching over you."

Instead, Jesus said something that utterly baffled His disciples:

"Our friend Lazarus sleeps, but I go that I may wake him up." (John 11:11)

The disciples, thinking with ordinary human logic, replied, **"Lord, if he sleeps he will get well."** They thought Jesus was speaking of natural, restorative slumber. But the text tells us Jesus was speaking of his death.

Then, Jesus did something profoundly important. He did not leave them in a confusing metaphor. He spoke plainly, with absolute clarity:

"Lazarus is dead." (John 11:14)

Do you see the magnificent, logical equivalence the Master established? In the mind of Jesus Christ, **death is sleep**. He did not separate the two. He did not describe death as a conscious journey to another realm. He described it as a state of unconscious rest, from which a person must be **awakened**.

If Lazarus's conscious soul had immediately gone to heaven, Jesus' statement would have been a deception. Why tell the disciples He was going to "wake him up" if Lazarus was already awake and conscious in the presence of God? The only logical, biblical conclusion is that Lazarus was entirely unconscious, resting in the grave, awaiting the voice of the Son of God.

To understand the depth of this truth, we must look at the original language of the New Testament. The Greek word Jesus and the apostles used for this "sleep" of death is **Koimao** (κοιμάω).

This is not a word used for a brief nap. In the biblical context, **Koimao** signifies a deep, temporary slumber from which one is expected to wake. In fact, this beautiful Greek root is where we get the English word "cemetery." The original Greek word for a burial place is **Koimeterion** (κοιμητήριον), which literally translates to "a sleeping place."

The early Christians did not call graveyards "places of the dead" or "realms of the departed." They called them sleeping places. Why? Because they understood the Master's teaching. The body is not a discarded shell; it is a resting traveler, waiting for the morning call.

This was not a unique metaphor used only by Jesus. The Holy Spirit inspired the apostles to adopt this exact terminology as the standard, theological description of death for all believers. Let us examine the evidence with clear, critical thinking.

When the first Christian martyr, Stephen, was being stoned to death, he did not cry out that his soul was flying to heaven. The Scripture records his final moment with profound peace:

"And when he had said this, he fell asleep." (Acts 7:60)

The Greek text uses the past tense of our word: **Ekoimēthē** (ἐκοιμήθη) — he fell asleep.

The Apostle Paul, writing to the Corinthians, refers to the hundreds of eyewitnesses of the resurrected Christ, noting that many are still alive, **"but some have fallen asleep"** (1 Corinthians 15:6). The Greek participle used here is **Kekoimēmenoi** (κεκοιμημένοι), meaning "those who are sleeping."

Paul uses this same comforting language to address the grieving church in Thessalonica, giving us one of the most emotionally resonant passages in all of Scripture regarding grief:

"But I do not want you to be ignorant, brethren, concerning those who have fallen asleep, lest you sorrow as others who have no hope. For if we believe that Jesus died and rose again, even so God will bring with Him those who sleep in Jesus." (1 Thessalonians 4:13-14)

Notice the practical, comforting logic Paul applies. He says we should not grieve **"as others who have no hope."** Why do the world grieve with hopeless despair? Because they believe death is a permanent, terrifying severance, or they are confused by myths of ghostly wandering.

But the believer's grief is different. It is a grief anchored in hope. Why? Because we know that those who have **"fallen asleep"** (**Koimōmenous** - κοιμωμένους) are not lost in a void. They are resting securely in the care of the Master, awaiting the day He returns to wake them.

Let us make this profoundly clear with an analogy that a twelve-year-old can easily grasp, yet holds deep intellectual weight for the wisest scholar.

Imagine a weary traveler who has walked a long, difficult journey through a harsh, stormy wilderness. The traveler is exhausted, bruised, and in pain. Finally, they reach a beautiful, secure inn. The innkeeper gently ushers them into a warm, quiet room, tucks them into a soft bed, and turns off the light. The traveler falls into a deep, dreamless sleep.

While the traveler sleeps, do they know about the storm raging outside? No. Do they feel the pain of their journey? No. Are they consciously waiting, checking their watch, anxious about the morning? No. They are in a state of perfect, unconscious rest, completely safe under the innkeeper's protection, simply waiting for the morning sun to rise and the innkeeper to gently wake them.

This is the biblical reality of death for the believer. The storm of this world—with its sickness, sorrow, and pain—ceases the moment the breath departs. The believer does not consciously endure the decay of the grave. They do not float as a ghost. They enter the **Koimeterion**, the sleeping place, preserved perfectly in the mind of God until the glorious morning of the resurrection.

Why is this truth so practically valuable for you today?

Because it liberates you from the anxiety of "signs" and "visitations." If a loved one has passed, you do not need to wonder if they are cold, lonely, or trying to send you confusing messages from the other side. They are not. They are resting. The silence of the grave is not a sign of abandonment; it is the seal of God's perfect peace.

Furthermore, it protects you from the dangerous deceptions of spiritualism. Since the dead are truly asleep, any "spirit" that claims to be your departed loved one, speaking to you through a medium or a Ouija board, is by biblical definition a counterfeit. The dead cannot speak. Only the living God can wake the dead.

Jesus called it sleep. The apostles called it sleep. The original Greek calls it a sleeping place.

Therefore, let us cast aside the terrifying myths of human tradition. Let us embrace the Master's terminology. Death is not a haunting; it is a holy pause. It is not the end of the story; it is merely the closing of the eyes, waiting for the triumphant, life-giving voice of the Son of God to say, **"Awake, and arise from the dead."**

As we turn the page, we must confront a sobering reality. If the dead are truly asleep and silent, then where do the "ghosts," "apparitions," and "voices of the dead" in our world actually come from? We must expose the great deception that seeks to counterfeit the Master's peaceful sleep.

PART III: THE GREAT DECEPTION

(Cultural Timing; Intellectual Depth; Warning against Spiritualism)

Chapter 7: Why God Forbids Talking to the Dead

- **Description:** A logical and scriptural defense of **Deuteronomy 18:10-12** and **Leviticus 19:31**. If the dead could talk to us, God would not strictly forbid it under penalty of death. The prohibition exists precisely because the dead **cannot** speak; therefore, any "spirit" claiming to be a deceased loved one is, by biblical definition, a deception.

My beloved child, let us reason together.

There is no ache in the human experience quite like the silence left behind by a departed loved one. In the quiet hours of the night, the heart cries out with a desperate, universal longing: **I just want to hear their voice one more time. I just want to know they are okay.**

In our modern age, this deep emotional vulnerability is heavily exploited. We see a cultural surge in "grief-tech," AI voice-cloning of the deceased, psychic mediums, and spiritualist practices that promise to bridge the gap between the living and the dead. It sounds so comforting. It feels so real.

But we must not allow our profound grief to blind us to the absolute truth of the Creator's design. We must apply clear, critical, and uncompromising logic. We must ask the most sensible, grounding question a truth-seeker can ask: **"Ano ang sabi ng Biblia?"** (What does the Bible actually say?)

When we turn to the unadulterated Word of God, we find a command that is absolute, severe, and non-negotiable.

Listen to the words of the Almighty through Moses in **Deuteronomy 18:10-12**:

"There shall not be found among you anyone who... practices witchcraft, or a soothsayer, or one who interprets omens, or a sorcerer, or one who conjures spells, or a medium (**Ov** - אוֹב), or a spiritist (**Yiddeoni** - יִדְּעֹנִי), or one who calls up the dead (**Doresh el-hammethim** - דֹּרֵשׁ אֶל-הַמֵּתִים). For all who do these things are an abomination to the Lord."

The prohibition is repeated with equal force in **Leviticus 19:31**:

"Give no regard to mediums (**Ov**) and familiar spirits (**Yiddeoni**); do not seek them out, to be defiled by them: I am the Lord your God."

Let us pause and apply rigorous, clear thinking to this divine law.

God is a loving Father. He is the author of family, of connection, and of comfort. If your child is in the next room, does a loving father strictly forbid you from speaking to them, under penalty of death? Of course not. A loving father only forbids an action if that action is inherently dangerous, harmful, or based on a lie.

Therefore, we must arrive at a profound, inescapable logical conclusion: **God strictly forbids consulting the dead precisely because the dead cannot speak.**

If the traditional myth were true—if the souls of the departed were consciously floating around, fully aware, and capable of communicating with the living—then God's command would be cruel, arbitrary, and illogical. Why would a loving God sever the natural bond between a grieving mother and her departed child, if that child were truly able to offer comfort from heaven?

But God is not cruel, and His Word is not illogical. The prohibition exists as a divine firewall. It exists to protect you.

If the dead are truly asleep in the silent archives of the grave, as we have thoroughly established from Ecclesiastes, Psalms, and the teachings of Jesus, then **who** is the entity speaking through a medium, a Ouija board, or a supposed "visitation"?

The Bible gives us a chillingly clear answer. If it is not your departed loved one, it is, by biblical definition, a deception.

The Apostle Paul warns us in **1 Timothy 4:1**:

"Now the Spirit expressly says that in latter times some will depart from the faith, giving heed to deceiving spirits and doctrines of demons."

The original Greek word for "deceiving" here is **Planos** (πλάνος), meaning misleading, fraudulent, or wandering. The Scripture explicitly identifies these communicating entities not as human souls, but as **Pneumata** (πνεύματα) of demons.

Furthermore, in **2 Corinthians 11:14**, we are given the master key to understanding these phenomena:

"And no wonder! For Satan himself transforms himself into an angel of light."

Let us make this profoundly clear with an analogy that a twelve-year-old can easily grasp, yet holds deep intellectual weight for the wisest scholar.

Imagine a young child sleeping safely in their bed upstairs. Suddenly, in the middle of the night, a voice calls out from the dark woods outside the window: **"Come outside, it's me, your father. I need you."**

The voice sounds exactly like the father. It knows the father's name. It uses the father's tone. But the child, if they are wise, will remember one crucial fact: **My father is safely asleep in his bed upstairs.**

Therefore, who is at the window? It is not the father. It is a wolf, mimicking the father's voice to lure the child into danger. The wise child does not open the window. The wise child locks it tighter and calls out to the true father in the next room for protection.

This is the exact spiritual reality of our world. Your departed loved one is safely "asleep" in the loving, protective memory of God. They are not wandering the earth. They are not trapped in a medium's parlor. They are at perfect rest.

Therefore, any "spirit" that knocks on the door of your mind, claiming to be your grandmother, your child, or your friend, is an imposter. It is a demonic entity exploiting your grief, using stolen memories and familiar mannerisms to deceive you, defile your faith, and lead you away from the true God.

This is why the penalty in the Old Testament was so severe. It was not because God was angry at people for loving their dead. It was because God knew that opening the door to the occult is opening the door to spiritual predators. He forbids it to **save** you.

This truth offers immense practical value and emotional liberation.

First, it frees you from the guilt of not "hearing" from your loved ones. You are not being ignored. They are not upset with you. They are simply resting, as God designed.

Second, it gives you the spiritual authority to reject any occult practice, no matter how "comforting" it seems. You can confidently say, **"My loved one is asleep in Christ. I will not consult the dead, for I serve the God of the living."**

The silence of the grave is not a void to be filled with psychic chatter. It is a sacred sanctuary, guarded by the Almighty. Do not let the wolves of deception mimic the voices of those you love. Keep the window locked. Rest in the truth.

As we turn the page, we will examine the most famous "ghost story" ever told, and use the razor-sharp light of biblical logic to expose how a single parable has been tragically misused to fuel the myth of conscious torment.

Chapter 8: Angels of Light and Familiar Spirits

- **Description:** Exposes the true source of "ghostly" apparitions and mediumship. Using **2 Corinthians 11:14** (Satan masquerading as an angel of light) and **1 Timothy 4:1** (deceiving spirits), this chapter reveals that necromancy and spiritualism are not interactions with human souls, but demonic counterfeits designed to lead humanity away from the truth of the resurrection.

My beloved child, let us reason together with absolute clarity.

We have established a profound, unshakable biblical truth: the dead are asleep. They are not floating as conscious ghosts, they are not watching us from the clouds, and they are not suffering in a fiery underworld. They are resting in the silent, peaceful archives of the grave, awaiting the resurrection.

But this undeniable truth forces us to confront a very real, very unsettling question that plagues our modern age: **If the dead are truly asleep, then who—or what—is speaking through mediums, psychics, Ouija boards, and supposed "ghostly apparitions"?**

We live in a cultural moment obsessed with the supernatural. Television shows, viral videos, and an entire industry of "grief counselors" and spiritualists promise to connect you with your departed loved ones. They offer specific details, familiar voices, and comforting messages. It feels real. It feels miraculous.

But we must not allow our deep emotional longing to override our critical thinking. We must anchor ourselves to the razor-sharp logic of the Scriptures and ask the most vital question: **"Ano ang sabi ng Biblia?"** (What does the Bible actually say?)

The Bible does not leave us in the dark about this phenomenon. It exposes the true source of these "ghostly" encounters with chilling precision. They are not the souls of the departed. They are demonic counterfeits.

Let us examine the master key to understanding spiritual deception, given to us by the Apostle Paul in **2 Corinthians 11:14**:

"And no wonder! For Satan himself transforms himself into an angel of light."

Let us look at the original Greek text. The word used for "transforms" is **Metaschematizetai** (μετασχηματίζεται). It means to change one's form, to disguise, or to masquerade. The enemy does not typically appear as a terrifying, horned monster. That would be too obvious. Instead, Satan disguises himself as an **Angelos Phōtos** (ἄγγελος φωτός)—an "angel of light." He mimics goodness, comfort, and familiarity to gain your trust.

How does this deception work in practice? The Apostle Paul warns us again in **1 Timothy 4:1**:

"Now the Spirit expressly says that in latter times some will depart from the faith, giving heed to deceiving spirits and doctrines of demons."

The Greek phrase for "deceiving spirits" is **Pneumasin Planois** (πνεύμασιν πλάνοις), and "doctrines of demons" is **Didaskaliais Daimoniōn** (διδασκαλίαις δαιμονίων). These are intelligent, malicious spiritual entities whose sole purpose is to lead humanity away from the truth of God and the hope of the resurrection.

To understand how this works, let us use an analogy that a twelve-year-old can easily grasp, yet holds deep intellectual weight for the wisest scholar.

Imagine you are at home, and the phone rings. You answer, and you hear a voice that sounds **exactly** like your mother. It knows your name. It knows the name of your childhood pet. It even knows a secret joke only the two of you share. The voice says, **"I am in trouble. I need you to give me the password to your bank account right now."**

Your heart races. The voice is so convincing. But then, your critical thinking kicks in. You remember one undeniable fact: **Your mother is safely asleep in her bed in the next room.**

Therefore, who is on the phone? Is it your mother? No. It is a thief, a hacker, using a "deepfake" or voice-mimicking technology to steal from you. The thief uses stolen, true information to build false trust.

This is the exact mechanism of a "familiar spirit." In the Old Testament, the Hebrew word for a medium or one who consults familiar spirits is **Ov** (אוֹב). An **Ov** is a spirit that acts like a ventriloquist, whispering familiar, intimate details to deceive the living. These demonic entities observe human lives. They listen. They gather memories, habits, and names. Then, when a grieving heart is vulnerable and seeking contact, these spirits step onto the stage, wearing the "mask" of the departed, using stolen knowledge to convince you they are your loved one.

Why do they do this? What is their ultimate goal?

Their goal is not just to scare you; their goal is to **replace** your faith in the resurrection of Jesus Christ with faith in the occult. If you believe you can talk to the dead, you no longer need the Savior who conquered death. If you believe your loved one is already a conscious spirit in heaven, you no longer need the biblical hope of the future resurrection. Spiritualism is a direct, calculated attack on the Gospel of Christ.

This is why the Bible gives us a powerful, practical command for spiritual self-defense in **1 John 4:1**:

"Beloved, do not believe every spirit, but test the spirits (Dokimazete ta pneumata - **δοκιμάζετε τὰ πνεύματα), whether they are of God; because many false prophets have gone out into the world."**

The Greek word **Dokimazete** means to examine, to prove, or to put to the test. How do we test a spirit? We test it against the unadulterated Word of God.

If a "spirit" claims to be your departed grandfather, but it contradicts the clear biblical teaching that the dead are asleep (Ecclesiastes 9:5), it fails the test. If it encourages you to seek guidance from the dead rather than from God through prayer, it fails the test. Any spirit that does not confess that Jesus Christ is the only way, the truth, and the life (John 14:6) is, by biblical definition, a spirit of antichrist (1 John 4:3).

This truth is not meant to terrify you; it is meant to **liberate** you.

Think of the immense practical value of this knowledge. You no longer have to live in fear of the dark, wondering if a ghost is in your house. You no longer have to feel guilty because you haven't "heard" from your departed loved one. You no longer have to be vulnerable to the manipulative, expensive, and spiritually dangerous traps of mediums and psychics.

You can stand firm, lock the door of your heart against deception, and declare: **"My loved one is resting in the peaceful sleep of the Lord. I will not consult the dead, for I serve the God of the living. I will not be deceived by familiar spirits, for I have the Holy Spirit and the sure promise of the resurrection."**

The voices of the occult are not the whispers of your ancestors. They are the echoes of the enemy, masquerading in the dark. But you are a child of the Light. You have the truth. And as Jesus Himself declared, **"You shall know the truth, and the truth shall make you free"** (John 8:32).

As we turn the page, we will address the single most misused passage in the entire Bible regarding the afterlife. We will take the famous story of the Rich Man and Lazarus, strip away centuries of human tradition, and use the light of biblical logic to prove once and for all that it is a parable, not a map of the afterlife.

Chapter 9: The Rich Man and Lazarus: Parable, Not Geography

- **Description:** A masterful, scholarly exegesis of **Luke 16:19-31**. Explains why this is a parable (using familiar Jewish folklore imagery to make a point about ignoring the Law and the Prophets) and not a literal map of the afterlife. Proves that if taken literally, it would contradict the clear, plain teachings of Ecclesiastes, Psalms, and Jesus' own words about the unconscious state of the dead.

My beloved child, let us reason together.

If you have ever discussed the afterlife with someone who firmly believes in the immortal soul and eternal conscious torment, you have undoubtedly heard this argument. They will open their Bible, point to Luke chapter 16, and say with absolute confidence: **"Here it is. Jesus Himself described a rich man suffering in flames and a poor man resting in Abraham's bosom. This is the literal map of the afterlife."**

It sounds definitive. It sounds final. But we must not read the Scriptures with a superficial glance. We must apply clear, critical, and uncompromising logic. We must ask the most sensible, grounding question a truth-seeker can ask: **"Ano ang talagang ibig sabihin nito?"** (What does this **really** mean?)

To understand this passage, we must let the Bible interpret the Bible. God is not the author of confusion (1 Corinthians 14:33). Therefore, a single passage cannot contradict the clear, plain, and repeated teachings of the rest of Scripture.

Let us read the text in **Luke 16:19-31**. It tells of a certain rich man, dressed in purple and fine linen, who feasted sumptuously every day. At his gate lay a beggar named Lazarus, full of sores, desiring to be fed with the crumbs from the rich man's table. Both men die. Lazarus is carried by angels to "Abraham's bosom," while the rich man is in "Hades," lifted up in torment. The rich man begs Abraham to send Lazarus to dip his finger in water to cool his tongue, and later, to warn his five living brothers. Abraham replies that they have "Moses and the prophets," and if they do not hear them, "neither will they be persuaded though one rise from the dead."

Now, let us apply rigorous, clear thinking. If we take this story as a literal, historical account of the afterlife, we create catastrophic contradictions with the rest of the Bible.

Contradiction 1: The Conscious Dead.

If this is literal, the dead are fully conscious, feeling pain, remembering their past, speaking, and seeing across a great gulf. But we have already established from **Ecclesiastes 9:5** that "the dead know nothing," and from **Psalm 146:4** that their thoughts perish. We know from **John 11:11-14** that Jesus Himself called death a "sleep." A literal reading of Luke 16 shatters the harmonious testimony of the entire Bible.

Contradiction 2: The Location of the Patriarchs.

In the story, Abraham is in "Hades" (the grave), yet he is conscious and comforting Lazarus. But the Apostle Peter, speaking under the inspiration of the Holy Spirit, declared clearly in **Acts 2:29, 34**: **"Men and brethren, let me speak freely to you of the patriarch David,**

that he is both dead and buried, and his tomb is with us to this day... For David did not ascend into the heavens." If David, a man after God's own heart, is still in his tomb, how much more Abraham? The patriarchs are asleep in the grave, awaiting the resurrection, not consciously hosting guests in the afterlife.

Contradiction 3: The Resurrection of Christ.

The rich man asks for someone to rise from the dead to warn his brothers. If this were a literal geography of heaven and hell, the rich man would be asking for someone to travel from "Abraham's bosom" (heaven) to earth. But **John 3:13** states unequivocally: **"No one has ascended to heaven but He who came down from heaven, that is, the Son of Man."**

How do we resolve this? The answer is found in the very first word of our analysis: This is not a literal history. It is a **parable**.

Let us look at the original Greek text. The word Jesus used for this type of story is **Parabole** (παραβολή). It means a placing beside, a comparison, or a fictional story used to illustrate a moral or spiritual truth. In **Matthew 13:34**, the Bible gives us a universal rule for understanding Jesus' teaching method: **"All these things Jesus spoke to the multitude in parables; and without a parable He did not speak to them."**

But why would Jesus tell a story that sounds so much like a popular myth? To understand this, we must look at the context. Just two verses earlier, **Luke 16:14** sets the stage:

"Now the Pharisees, who were lovers of money, also heard all these things, and they derided Him."

Jesus is speaking **directly** to the Pharisees. In the first century, there was a well-known Jewish folk tale circulating among the people about a rich, arrogant man and a poor, righteous beggar named Lazarus (from the Hebrew **Eleazar** - אֶלְעָזָר, meaning "God helps").

Jesus did not invent these characters. He hijacked a familiar story that the Pharisees already knew, but He radically changed the ending to deliver a devastating, prophetic critique of **their** greed and **their** rejection of God's Word.

In the folk tale, the rich man was usually punished for his cruelty. But Jesus' audience would have assumed the rich man in the story represented the blessed, wealthy Pharisees, and the beggar represented the cursed, sinful outcasts. Jesus flipped the script. He showed that in God's economy, the humble, suffering faithful (like the tax collectors and sinners Jesus was welcoming) are the ones comforted by God, while the arrogant, money-loving religious leaders who ignore the poor will face divine reversal.

The climax of the story is not a lesson about the geography of the afterlife. The climax is a piercing warning to the living, found in **Luke 16:31**:

"But he said to him, 'If they do not hear Moses and the prophets, neither will they be persuaded though one rise from the dead.'"

Do you see the brilliant, intellectual depth of the Master Teacher? Jesus was prophesying His own resurrection. He was telling the Pharisees: **"You have the Scriptures (Moses and the Prophets). They tell you to love God and love your neighbor. If you reject the plain Word of God, even if I, the Messiah, rise from the dead, you still will not believe Me."**

And history proved Him right. Jesus **did** rise from the dead. The Pharisees were told about it. Yet, they bribed the guards to say His body was stolen (Matthew 28:11-15). They rejected the ultimate miracle because their hearts were already hardened against the truth of Moses and the Prophets.

Let us make this profoundly clear with an analogy that a twelve-year-old can easily grasp, yet holds deep intellectual weight for the wisest scholar.

Imagine a modern teacher wants to warn her students about the dangers of texting while driving. She knows they won't listen to a dry lecture. So, she tells a story: **"Imagine a superhero, like Spider-Man, who gets a text message while swinging through the city, gets distracted, and crashes into a building."**

Now, if a student raises their hand and says, **"But teacher, Spider-Man isn't real, and he doesn't use a smartphone!"** the teacher would reply, **"I know. I am using a fictional character you recognize to teach you a very real lesson about distraction and safety."**

The details of the story (Spider-Man, smartphones) are not literal facts; they are the **vehicle** for the truth. The **truth** is the danger of distracted driving.

In the same way, the details of the rich man and Lazarus (conscious conversation in Hades, Abraham's bosom) are not literal geography. They are the familiar, fictional vehicle Jesus used to deliver a very real, urgent truth to the Pharisees: **Hear the Scriptures, or you will perish in your unbelief.**

Why is this truth so practically valuable for you today?

Because it liberates you from the fear of a cruel, torturous God. It protects you from the theological trap of using a single, misunderstood parable to overthrow the clear, plain, and repeated teachings of the entire Bible regarding the peaceful, unconscious sleep of the dead.

When you read the Bible with clear thinking, allowing Scripture to interpret Scripture, the harmony of God's Word sings. The dead are asleep. They are not burning. They are not consciously waiting. They are resting in the promise of the resurrection. And the story of the Rich Man and Lazarus stands not as a map of the afterlife, but as a timeless, urgent warning to the living: **Listen to the Word of God today, for it is the only true guide to eternal life.**

As we turn the page, we will step out of the shadows of deception and into the glorious, triumphant light of the Resurrection, where we will discover the breathtaking power of the One who holds the keys of death and Hades.

PART IV: THE GREAT AWAKENING

(Universal Themes of Hope and Freedom; Aesthetic Beauty of the Resurrection Promise)

Chapter 10: The Voice That Shatters the Silence

- **Description:** The triumphant turning point of the book. Explores **John 5:25** and **John 11:25**. The dead do not wake themselves up. They await the **phonē** (φωνή - voice) of the Son of God. Christ holds the keys of death and Hades (Revelation 1:18). Our hope is not in ghosts, but in the resurrected Savior.

My beloved child, let us reason together.

We have journeyed through the shadows of human tradition and emerged into the clear, liberating light of biblical truth. We have seen that the soul is not an immortal ghost. We have seen that the grave is not a place of conscious torment or ghostly wandering, but a state of deep, dreamless, and peaceful slumber.

But if the dead are truly asleep, and the grave is utterly silent, a profound and vital question arises: **How does the story end?**

If death is merely a sleep, then sleep implies an awakening. And this is where the narrative of human history pivots from a tragedy of silence into a symphony of triumphant hope. We now arrive at the very heart of the Gospel. Our hope is not found in the myths of floating spirits, but in the absolute, universe-shattering power of the Resurrected Savior.

Let us ask the most sensible, grounding question a truth-seeker can ask: **"Ano ang sabi ng Biblia?"** (What does the Bible actually say about how the dead are awakened?)

The Master Teacher, our Lord Jesus Christ, did not leave us with vague philosophies about the afterlife. Standing before the tomb of His dear friend Lazarus, He made a declaration that echoes through the corridors of eternity. In **John 11:25**, He said:

"I am the resurrection and the life. He who believes in Me, though he may die, he shall live."

Let us examine the original Greek text. Jesus declares, **"Ego eimi hē anastasis kai hē zōē"** (ἐγώ εἰμι ἡ ἀνάστασις καὶ ἡ ζωή). He does not say, "I know the way to the resurrection." He says, **"I AM"** the resurrection. The Greek word for resurrection, **Anastasis** (ἀνάστασις), literally means "a standing up again." Jesus is the very power, the very source, and the very event of standing up again from the sleep of death.

But how does this awakening happen? Does the sleeping soul somehow gather its strength and wake itself up? Does it float out of the grave on its own?

Absolutely not. A sleeping person cannot wake themselves up by sheer willpower. They require an external stimulus. They require a voice.

Jesus explains the exact mechanics of this glorious event in **John 5:25**:

"Most assuredly, I say to you, the hour is coming and now is, when the dead will hear the voice (phonē - **φωνή**) **of the Son of God; and those who hear will live."**

Notice the profound logic here. The dead will **hear** the **phonē** (φωνή). Now, you might ask, **"But if the dead are unconscious and know nothing, as Ecclesiastes 9:5 says, how can they hear?"**

This is where the divine logic of the Creator surpasses human understanding. The voice of the Son of God is not merely a sound wave traveling through the air. It is the same creative, life-giving power that spoke the universe into existence in Genesis 1. When God said, **"Let there be light,"** the light did not exist beforehand to hear the command; the command **created** the light.

In the same way, the **phonē** of Christ is the creative spark that simultaneously awakens the sleeper and restores the life. The dead do not hear the voice **while** they are asleep; the voice of the Son of God is the very power that breaks the sleep, restores the **Ruach** (רוּחַ - breath of life), and causes them to hear and live in that very instant.

To make this profoundly clear, let us use an analogy that a twelve-year-old can easily grasp, yet holds deep intellectual weight for the wisest scholar.

Imagine a magnificent, ancient vault built into the side of a mountain. Inside this vault, a weary traveler lies in a deep, perfectly peaceful sleep. The vault is locked with an impenetrable, divine mechanism. The traveler cannot hear the storms raging outside. They cannot feel the passage of time. They cannot wake themselves up, nor can any human force, no matter how strong, break the lock.

The traveler is entirely dependent on one thing: the return of the Master of the vault, who alone possesses the key, and whose voice the traveler's heart recognizes.

When the Master returns, He does not shout for the traveler to wake up from the outside, hoping the sleeper might hear. The Master inserts the key, turns the lock, opens the door, and speaks a single, loving word. That word, combined with the opening of the door, instantly breaks the slumber. The traveler wakes up, not to fear, but to the face of the One who saved them.

This is the biblical reality of the resurrection. And who is this Master? The Apostle John, in his vision on the island of Patmos, saw the glorified, resurrected Jesus Christ and recorded His breathtaking claim in **Revelation 1:18**:

"I am He who lives, and was dead, and behold, I am alive forevermore. Amen. And I have the keys of Hades and of Death."

Let us look at the original Greek. Jesus says He holds the **Kleis** (κλεῖς - keys) of **Thanatos** (θάνατος - death) and **Hades** (ᾅδης - the grave or state of death).

In the ancient world, the person who held the keys to a city or a prison held absolute, undisputed authority over who entered and who left. By declaring that He holds the keys to Death and the Grave, Jesus is making a cosmic, undeniable claim: **No one enters the grave without His permission, and no one leaves the grave except by His command.**

Think about the immense practical value and emotional liberation of this truth.

In our modern age, humanity is desperately, frantically trying to "hack" death. We see a cultural obsession with cryogenics, uploading human consciousness to computers, and seeking immortality through science or the occult. We are terrified of the silence of the grave, so we try to build our own keys to unlock it.

But all human efforts are futile. Science cannot reverse the decay of the dust. Technology cannot restore the departed **Ruach**. Spiritualism only opens the door to deceiving spirits (**pneumasin planois** - πνεύμασιν πλάνοις), not to our loved ones.

The true, only hope for humanity is not found in human ingenuity. It is found in the nail-scarred hands of the One who already conquered the grave. Because Jesus died and rose again, He earned the right to hold the keys. Because He holds the keys, the grave is not a permanent prison; it is merely a temporary waiting room.

This truth transforms how we view our own mortality and the loss of our loved ones. We do not need to fear the silence of the cemetery. The silence is not empty; it is pregnant with the promise of the Master's return. We can stand by the graves of our believing loved ones, not with the hopeless despair of those who think they are gone forever, but with the confident, tearful joy of those who know the Master holds the key.

We know that one day, the archangel will shout, the trumpet of God will sound, and the **phonē** (φωνή) of the Son of God will shatter the silence of the ages. The dust will reassemble. The breath of life will return. And those who sleep in Jesus will rise, not as ghosts, but as glorified, immortal beings, forever united with their Savior.

Our hope is not in the myths of the departed. Our hope is in the Resurrected King.

As we turn the page, we will explore the breathtaking speed and power of this coming event, discovering how, in the twinkling of an eye, the mortal will put on immortality, and the promise of God will be fulfilled in glorious, undeniable reality.

Chapter 11: In the Twinkling of an Eye

- **Description:** A vivid, breathtaking description of the resurrection event based on **1 Corinthians 15:51-52** and **1 Thessalonians 4:16-17**. The trumpet sounds, the archangel calls, and the sleeping **nephesh** is instantly clothed with immortality and incorruption. This is the "blessed hope" that replaces the terror of death.

My beloved child, let us reason together.

We have journeyed through the silent, peaceful archives of the grave. We have established that death is not a terrifying, conscious wandering, but a deep, dreamless slumber. The sleeping **nephesh** (נֶפֶשׁ - living being) rests securely in the memory of the Creator.

But a profound question remains: If the dead are asleep in the decaying dust of the earth, how does God reverse this? Does He slowly coax the soul back into a rotting body? Does the awakening happen gradually, like a person slowly stirring from a nap?

The unadulterated Word of God gives us an answer so breathtaking, so powerful, and so instantaneous that it shatters every human fear of decay. The resurrection is not a slow process. It is a cosmic, instantaneous event of divine power.

Let us ask the most sensible, awe-inspiring question a truth-seeker can ask: **"Ano ang sabi ng Biblia?"** (What does the Bible actually say about the speed and power of the resurrection?)

The Apostle Paul, under the direct inspiration of the Holy Spirit, pulls back the curtain on this glorious event in his first letter to the Thessalonians. Listen to the majestic sequence of the awakening in **1 Thessalonians 4:16**:

"For the Lord Himself will descend from heaven with a shout, with the voice of an archangel, and with the trumpet of God. And the dead in Christ will rise first."

Notice the divine order. This is not a silent, passive event. It is a royal, triumphant arrival.

First, the **Keleusma** (κέλευσμα) — a loud shout of command, like a king rallying his troops or a captain commanding his ship.

Second, the **Phōnē Archangelou** (φωνὴ ἀρχαγγέλου) — the voice of the chief messenger, echoing across the cosmos.

Third, the **Salpinx** (σάλπιγξ) — the trumpet of God. In ancient Israel, the trumpet was not merely a musical instrument; it was the ultimate signal for assembly, for war, and for the arrival of the King.

When this divine symphony sounds, it penetrates the deepest, most silent grave. It is the ultimate wake-up call for the sleeping **nephesh**.

But how fast does this transformation occur? The Apostle Paul reveals this in one of the most thrilling passages in all of Scripture, found in **1 Corinthians 15:51-52**:

"Behold, I tell you a mystery (mysterion - **μυστήριον**)**: We shall not all sleep, but we shall all be changed— in a moment** (en atomō - **ἐν ἀτόμῳ**)**, in the twinkling of an eye** (en rhipē ophthalmou - **ἐν ῥιπῇ ὀφθαλμοῦ**)**, at the last trumpet. For the trumpet will sound, and the dead will be raised incorruptible** (aphthartoi - **ἄφθαρτοι**)**, and we shall be changed."**

Let us examine the original Greek with the precision of a scholar and the wonder of a child.

Paul calls this a **Mysterion** (μυστήριον). In the Bible, a mystery is not a confusing puzzle; it is a divine truth that was once hidden but is now revealed by God.

How fast will this happen? Paul uses two specific Greek phrases to describe the speed:

1. **En atomō** (ἐν ἀτόμῳ): This is where we get the English word "atom." In ancient Greek, it literally means "that which cannot be cut" or "an indivisible moment." It is the absolute smallest, most indivisible fraction of time conceivable.

2. **En rhipē ophthalmou** (ἐν ῥιπῇ ὀφθαλμοῦ): This translates to "in the twinkling of an eye" or "the flicker of an eyelid."

This is faster than a human heartbeat. It is faster than a nerve impulse traveling to the brain. It is instantaneous.

And what is the result of this instantaneous change? The dead are raised **Aphthartoi** (ἄφθαρτοι). This magnificent Greek word means "incorruptible," "imperishable," or "immune to decay." Furthermore, Paul states in verse 53 that this mortal body must put on **Athanasia** (ἀθανασία) — immortality.

To make this profoundly clear, let us use an analogy that a twelve-year-old can easily grasp, yet holds deep intellectual weight for the wisest scholar.

Imagine a young child building a beautiful, intricate sandcastle on the beach. For a while, it is magnificent. But soon, the tide comes in. The water begins to wash away the walls. The sand grows heavy, dark, and begins to collapse. The child watches, helpless, as their creation slowly decays and dissolves back into the ocean. This represents our mortal bodies, subject to aging, sickness, and the slow decay of the grave.

But now, imagine the Master Architect of the universe steps onto the beach. He does not just watch the sandcastle dissolve. He does not slowly try to rebuild it grain by grain. Instead, He raises His hand and speaks a single, powerful word of command.

In less than the blink of an eye (**en rhipē ophthalmou**), the water reverses. The scattered sand instantly flies back together. But it does not remain sand. In that indivisible moment (**en atomō**), the fragile, decaying sand is instantly transformed into a fortress of solid, brilliant, unbreakable diamond. The tide can never wash it away again. It is **aphthartos**—incorruptible.

This is the biblical reality of the resurrection. God does not merely "fix" our decaying bodies. He instantaneously transforms them. The dust is reassembled, the **Ruach** (רוּחַ - breath of life) is restored, and the mortal **nephesh** is instantly clothed in immortal, incorruptible glory.

Why is this truth so emotionally resonant and practically valuable for us today?

We live in a cultural age obsessed with fighting decay. Humanity spends billions of dollars on anti-aging creams, medical technologies, and even "transhumanist" dreams of uploading our minds to computers, all in a desperate, futile attempt to escape the decay of the grave. We are terrified of the fragility of our bodies.

But the believer has a superior, divine answer. We do not need to fear the wrinkles of age, the weakness of sickness, or the finality of the grave. Why? Because we possess what the Apostle Paul calls the **Elpis Makaria** (ἐλπὶς μακαρία) — the "blessed hope" (Titus 2:13).

This "blessed hope" is not a vague, wishful thinking that "things will get better." It is a confident, joyful, and absolute expectation based on the promise of the Resurrected King.

This truth completely transforms how we grieve. When we stand at the graveside of a loved one who slept in Jesus, we do not stare at the dirt with hopeless despair. We look at the horizon with holy anticipation. We know that the grave is not a permanent prison; it is merely a temporary cocoon. We know that the Master Architect is coming, and when His trumpet sounds, our loved one will not rise as a frail, decaying ghost, but as a glorious, incorruptible being, more alive than we can possibly imagine.

The Apostle Paul concludes his teaching on this magnificent event with a deeply practical command in **1 Thessalonians 4:18**:

"Therefore comfort one another with these words."

Not with empty platitudes. Not with myths of floating spirits. But with **these** words: The Lord will descend. The trumpet will sound. The dead will rise incorruptible. And we shall be changed.

Let this truth anchor your soul. The terror of death has been defeated. The decay of the grave is only temporary. In the twinkling of an eye, the silence will be shattered, the sleep will end, and the children of God will awake to an eternal, imperishable morning.

As we turn the page, we must face a sobering, yet necessary truth. The trumpet will sound for **everyone**. The graves will open for **all**. We will now explore the divine reality that there are two awakenings, leading to two very different, eternal destinies.

Chapter 12: Two Awakenings, Two Eternal Destinies

- **Description:** A sober, truthful look at **Daniel 12:2** and **John 5:29**. Not all who wake up will rejoice. There is a resurrection of life and a resurrection of judgment. Explores the biblical truth of the "second death" (**Revelation 20:14, 21:8**)—not eternal conscious torment, but complete, everlasting destruction (**apōleia** - ἀπώλεια) for those who reject God's grace, while the righteous inherit a new earth free from pain (Revelation 21:4).

My beloved child, let us reason together.

We have journeyed through the profound peace of the grave. We have seen that death is not a conscious torment, but a deep, dreamless sleep. We have marveled at the breathtaking promise that the trumpet of God will sound, and the sleeping **nephesh** (נֶפֶשׁ - living being) will be instantaneously clothed in immortality.

But logic, clear thinking, and the unadulterated Word of God demand that we ask a sobering, vital question: **When the trumpet sounds, does everyone who wakes up receive the same reward?**

The human heart desperately wants to believe that all roads lead to the same glorious destination. But the Master Teacher, who is the embodiment of Truth, never traded honesty for comfort. He spoke with absolute clarity about the reality of divine justice.

Let us ask the most critical question a truth-seeker can ask: **"Ano ang sabi ng Biblia?"** (What does the Bible actually say about the final awakening?)

The Prophet Daniel, granted a vision of the end of days, recorded a foundational truth in **Daniel 12:2**:

"And many of those who sleep in the dust of the earth shall awake (yaqitzu - **יָקִיצוּ**), **some to everlasting life** (chayyei olam - **חַיֵּי עוֹלָם**), **and some to shame and everlasting contempt** (deraon olam - **דִּרְאוֹן עוֹלָם**)."

Notice the profound, inescapable logic of this verse. The Hebrew word **Yaqitzu** means "shall awake." It confirms that both groups were **asleep** in the dust. If the wicked were already suffering in a fiery hell, they would not need to "awake" from the dust; they would already be awake in torment. The resurrection proves the sleep of the dead.

But upon awakening, their destinies diverge eternally. One group receives **Chayyei Olam** (everlasting life). The other receives **Deraon Olam**. The Hebrew word **Deraon** means horror, abhorrence, or utter shame. It is the profound, eternal realization of having rejected the Creator, resulting in permanent, irreversible loss.

Our Lord Jesus Christ confirmed this exact dichotomy. In **John 5:28-29**, He declared:

"Do not marvel at this; for the hour is coming in which all who are in the graves will hear His voice and come forth—those who have done good, to the resurrection of life (anastasis zōēs - ***ἀνάστασις ζωῆς***), **and those who have done evil, to the resurrection of condemnation** (anastasis kriseōs - ***ἀνάστασις κρίσεως***)."

Again, the logic is flawless. There are two resurrections. There is an **Anastasis Zōēs** (a standing up again to life) and an **Anastasis Kriseōs** (a standing up again to judgment or condemnation).

This brings us to the most misunderstood, and frankly, the most damaging doctrine in traditional theology: the concept of "eternal conscious torment." We have been taught to picture a God who, out of infinite love, nevertheless keeps human souls alive forever in a lake of fire to be tortured endlessly.

But we must apply critical thinking. Does this align with the character of God? The Apostle John wrote, **"God is love"** (1 John 4:8). A God who eternally tortures His creation is not a God of love; He is a cosmic sadist. Furthermore, we have already proven from Ezekiel 18:4 that "the soul who sins shall die." An immortal soul cannot die. Therefore, the traditional view contradicts the plain teaching of Scripture.

So, what is the "lake of fire"? What is the "second death"?

The Apostle John provides the definitive answer in **Revelation 21:8**:

"But the cowardly, unbelieving, abominable, murderers, sexually immoral, sorcerers, idolaters, and all liars shall have their part in the lake which burns with fire and brimstone, which is the second death."

And in **Revelation 20:14**:

"Then Death and Hades were cast into the lake of fire. This is the second death."

Let us examine the original Greek. The ultimate fate of the unrepentant is described by the word **Apōleia** (ἀπώλεια), which is translated as "destruction," "ruin," or "utter loss." It does not mean "preservation in torment." It means the complete and final cessation of existence.

To make this profoundly clear, let us use an analogy that a twelve-year-old can easily grasp, yet holds deep intellectual weight for the wisest scholar.

Imagine a beautiful garden. In this garden, there are vibrant, life-giving rose bushes, and there are also toxic, choking weeds that threaten to destroy the entire garden. The Master Gardener loves the garden. He does not want the weeds to remain.

When the Gardener removes the weeds, He does not keep them alive forever in a special "weed torture chamber" just to punish them. That would serve no purpose and would only perpetuate the toxicity. Instead, He pulls the weeds up by the roots and throws them into a fire.

What happens to the weed in the fire? It burns. It is consumed. And what is left? **Ashes.**

The Prophet Malachi describes this exact picture in **Malachi 4:1, 3**: **"For behold, the day is coming, burning like an oven... And you shall trample the wicked, for they shall be ashes under the soles of your feet."**

Ashes do not scream. Ashes do not feel pain. Ashes are the final, irreversible result of complete destruction. The fire is not eternal in its **process** (burning forever), but it is eternal in its **consequence** (once you are ashes, you are gone forever). This is the "second death." It is the merciful, just, and final eradication of sin and those who willingly cling to it. God does not torture; He cleanses.

Now, contrast this sobering reality with the breathtaking, emotionally resonant promise given to those who are found "in Christ."

For the righteous, the awakening is not to shame, but to an unprecedented, glorious reality. John describes it in **Revelation 21:4**:

"And God will wipe away every tear from their eyes; there shall be no more death (thanatos - **θάνατος**)**, nor sorrow** (penthos - **πένθος**)**, nor crying** (kraugē - **κραυγή**)**, nor there shall be any more pain** (ponos - **πόνος**)**, for the former things have passed away."**

The Greek word used for "new" in verse 1 ("a new heaven and a new earth") is **Kainos** (καινός). It does not just mean "new in time"; it means **new in quality**, fresh, unprecedented, and superior to anything that existed before.

Think about the practical, life-changing value of this truth.

First, it liberates you from the terror of a cruel, vindictive God. You can love God with your whole heart, knowing that His justice is perfect and His mercy is profound. He does not delight in the destruction of the wicked (Ezekiel 33:11); He takes no pleasure in it. But He will not allow sin to infect His new creation forever.

Second, it gives urgent, profound meaning to the choices you make **today**. The sleep of death is peaceful for everyone, but the awakening is determined by your relationship with the Resurrected King right now. You are either preparing for the **Anastasis Zōēs** (resurrection of life) or the **Anastasis Kriseōs** (resurrection of condemnation).

The grave is not the end of the story. It is merely the pause before the final chapter. And in that final chapter, there are only two destinies: the glorious, tearless, painless eternity of the New Earth, or the final, irreversible silence of the second death.

Which awakening will you prepare for?

As we turn the page, we will discover the only, infallible way to ensure you are numbered among those who will rise to everlasting life. We will explore the magnificent, unshakable assurance of being "in Christ," and how the true Church of God serves as the pillar and foundation of this saving truth.

PART V: THE GREAT ASSURANCE

(Practical Value; How to secure this hope today)

Chapter 13: No Condemnation in the Anointed One

- **Description:** Explores **Romans 8:1**. How does one ensure they are part of the first, glorious resurrection? By being "in Christ Jesus." This chapter explains the biblical mechanics of salvation: grace, faith, repentance, and the profound symbolism of baptism as a burial and resurrection with Him (Romans 6:4-5).

My beloved child, let us reason together.

We live in an age that carries a heavy, unspoken burden. On the surface, our culture preaches moral relativism: **"Do what feels right. Judge no one. There is no absolute right or wrong."** Yet beneath this modern veneer lies a deep, universal ache. The human conscience is not so easily silenced. We carry regret for words spoken, promises broken, secrets hidden, and paths chosen that led us away from light. We feel the quiet, gnawing weight of our own failures. And in the quiet of the night, the question whispers: **Will I ever be truly clean? Will I ever stand before a holy God without fear of judgment?**

Humanity has always tried to answer this question with self-effort. We build moral ladders. We perform good deeds. We seek religious rituals. We hope that if we simply try harder, the scales of heaven will tip in our favor.

But the unadulterated Word of God dismantles this exhausting, futile pursuit with a single, universe-altering declaration. The Apostle Paul, inspired by the Holy Spirit, delivers the most liberating legal verdict ever spoken to the human heart in **Romans 8:1**:

"There is therefore now no condemnation to those who are in Christ Jesus."

Let us examine this with the precision of a scholar and the wonder of a child. The original Greek text is breathtaking in its clarity. The word for "condemnation" is **Katakrima** (κατάκριμα). It is not a mild disappointment. It is a judicial term. It means a formal sentence of guilt, a legal penalty pronounced against a defendant who has broken the law.

Paul declares: **There is now no katakrima.**

Why? Because the verdict has already been served. The penalty has already been paid. The sentence has been lifted. But notice the crucial, non-negotiable condition attached to this freedom: **To those who are in Christ Jesus.**

The Greek phrase is **En Christō Iēsou** (ἐν Χριστῷ Ἰησοῦ). This is not merely a theological slogan. It is a spatial, relational, and covenantal reality. To be "in Christ" means to be united with Him, covered by His righteousness, and identified with His finished work. It is the divine equivalent of standing behind an impenetrable shield. The arrows of guilt, the verdicts of shame, and the accusations of the accuser cannot reach you, because you are hidden in Him.

But how, practically and biblically, does a person enter into this state? How do we move from the realm of **Katakrima** to the reality of being **En Christō**?

The Scriptures do not leave us guessing. They give us the exact, unadulterated mechanics of salvation. Let us trace the divine pathway with clear, logical thinking.

First: Grace (Charis - χάρις)

Salvation begins not with human effort, but with divine initiative. The Apostle Paul states in **Ephesians 2:8**: **"For by grace you have been saved through faith, and that not of yourselves; it is the gift of God."** The Greek word **Charis** means unmerited favor, a gift given freely, not earned. You cannot buy it. You cannot work for it. You can only receive it.

Second: Faith (Pistis - πίστις)

Grace is the gift; faith is the open hand that receives it. **Pistis** means trust, reliance, and confident surrender. It is not mere intellectual agreement that God exists. Even the demons believe and tremble (James 2:19). Biblical faith is leaning your entire weight upon the promise and character of Christ. It is saying, **"I cannot save myself. I trust You to do what You promised."**

Third: Repentance (Metanoia - μετάνοια)

Faith without repentance is incomplete. **Metanoia** is often translated as "repentance," but it literally means "a change of mind." It is a radical, decisive turn. It is not merely feeling sorry for getting caught. It is a conscious, willful reversal: turning **away** from the path of self-rule and sin, and turning **toward** the path of God's truth and righteousness. As Jesus commanded in Luke 13:3, **"Unless you repent, you will all likewise perish."** Repentance is the door through which faith steps into obedience.

Fourth: Baptism (Baptisma - βάπτισμα)

Here is where many traditional teachings grow vague, but the original text is stunningly clear. How does one practically enter into union with Christ? The Apostle Paul answers in **Romans 6:3-5**:

"Or do you not know that as many of us as were baptized into Christ Jesus were baptized into His death? Therefore we were buried with Him through baptism into death, that just as Christ was raised from the dead by the glory of the Father, even so we also should walk in newness of life. For if we have been united together

in the likeness of His death, we shall certainly also be in the likeness of His resurrection."

Notice the Greek verb for "buried with Him": **Syntaphēmen** (συνετάφημεν). The prefix **syn-** means "together with." Baptism is not a mere sprinkling of water on an infant's forehead. The root word **Baptizō** (βαπτίζω) literally means to immerse, to dip, to submerge completely.

Let us make this profoundly clear with an analogy that a twelve-year-old can easily grasp, yet holds deep intellectual weight for the wisest scholar.

Imagine a person standing on the shore of a vast, calm sea. The shore represents the old life: the guilt, the regret, the self-directed path, the condemnation. The person cannot wash themselves clean by standing on the sand and scrubbing their hands. The dirt is too deep.

So, the person steps into the water. They do not dip a toe. They do not sprinkle a few drops. They are fully immersed. They go under the surface. In that moment, the water covers them completely. The shore disappears. The old life is left behind, symbolically buried beneath the waves.

Then, they rise. They break the surface, gasping, dripping, breathing fresh air. They step onto the opposite shore. They are a new person. The water did not create the newness, but it marked the undeniable transition. It was the moment of passage from death to life, from burial to resurrection.

This is the biblical reality of baptism. It is not a human ritual for show. It is a sacred, obedient act of identification. When you are immersed in water in the name of Jesus Christ, you are publicly declaring: **"My old self is crucified with Him. My past is buried. I am rising to walk in newness of life."** The Apostle Peter calls it the answer of a good conscience toward God (1 Peter 3:21). It is the moment you step out of the courtroom of guilt and into the family of the Father.

Why is this truth so emotionally resonant and practically valuable today?

Because it destroys the paralyzing cycle of performance-based religion. You will never earn your way into being "in Christ." But you can step into Him today. Through grace, through faith, through a genuine change of mind, and through obedient baptism, the legal record of your sins is nailed to the cross (Colossians 2:14). The verdict shifts from **Katakrima** (condemnation) to **Dikaioma** (δικαίωμα - righteous decree).

This does not mean you will never struggle with temptation. It does not mean you will never make mistakes. But it means you will never again face those failures under the crushing weight of condemnation. When you fall, you do not run away from God; you run **to** Him, because you know your standing is not based on your performance, but on your position in the Anointed One.

"There is now no condemnation."

Let those words sink into your soul. The guilt you have carried is not your final identity. The shame you have hidden is not your eternal destiny. You can step into the water of obedience today, rise with Christ tomorrow, and live forever in the glorious, unshakable freedom of being His.

As we turn the page, we will address a vital question that naturally follows: **If being "in Christ" is the only way to the resurrection of life, where is He to be found today?** We will discover that Christ did not leave His truth scattered across a thousand conflicting traditions, but established one pillar, one foundation, one living assembly to guard the path to eternal life.

Chapter 14: The Pillar and Foundation of Truth

- **Description:** A vital, sensible, and direct exposition on the Church. Cites **1 Timothy 3:15** and **1 Corinthians 1:1-2**. Christ did not leave His truth to be scattered among thousands of conflicting traditions. He established His **Ekklēsia** (ἐκκλησία - the called-out assembly), the Church of God, as the sole pillar and ground of the truth. To be "in Christ" is to be aligned with the teachings and practices of His true Church.

My beloved child, let us reason together.

We live in an age of overwhelming noise. If you open a search engine or walk into a bookstore, you will find thousands of voices, each claiming to hold the secret to God, the meaning of life, and the path to eternity. We are told, **"Follow your own truth,"** or **"All paths lead to the same mountain."** It sounds tolerant. It sounds peaceful.

But let us apply clear, critical, and uncompromising logic. If there are thousands of paths, and they all contradict one another, they cannot all be true. A map that says "go north" and another that says "go south" cannot both lead to the same destination. God is not the author of confusion (1 Corinthians 14:33). Therefore, truth, by its very nature, must be singular, unified, and anchored.

When the Master Teacher, our Lord Jesus Christ, walked this earth, He did not leave His divine truth scattered like seeds in the wind, hoping human tradition would eventually piece it together. He established a specific, visible, and unshakable structure to guard, proclaim, and preserve His Word until the end of the age.

We must ask the most sensible, grounding question a truth-seeker can ask: **"Ano ang sabi ng Biblia?"** (What does the Bible actually say about where truth resides today?)

The Apostle Paul, writing under the direct inspiration of the Holy Spirit, gives us the definitive answer in **1 Timothy 3:15**:

"But if I am delayed, I write so that you may know how you ought to conduct yourself in the house of God, which is the church of the living God, the pillar and ground of the truth."

Let us examine the original Greek text with the precision of a scholar and the wonder of a child.

Paul describes the Church using three profound Greek terms:

1. **Ekklēsia** (ἐκκλησία): This is the word translated as "church." It is formed from two words: **ek** (out of) and **kaleō** (to call). It literally means "the called-out assembly." It is not a building of brick and mortar. It is a specific people, called out from the world by God, to belong to Him.

2. **Stylos** (στῦλος): This means "pillar." In ancient architecture, a pillar was not merely decorative. It was the essential, vertical structure that held up the entire roof. Without the pillar, the building collapses.

3. **Hedraiōma** (ἑδραίωμα): This means "ground," "foundation," or "bulwark." It is the solid, unmovable base upon which the pillar stands.

Do you see the magnificent, logical picture Paul is painting? The truth of God is not a floating, subjective idea. It is a massive, divine structure. The **Ekklēsia** (the Church of the living God) is the **Stylos** (the pillar) and the **Hedraiōma** (the foundation) that holds up and displays the truth to a dark world.

If you want to know the truth, you do not look to the shifting sands of human philosophy, popular culture, or personal feelings. You look to the pillar. You look to the Church that Christ built.

The Apostle Paul reinforces this exact identity in his opening greeting to the Corinthians in **1 Corinthians 1:1-2**:

"Paul, called to be an apostle of Jesus Christ through the will of God... To the church of God (Ekklēsia tou Theou - **ἐκκλησίᾳ τοῦ Θεοῦ) which is at Corinth, to those who are sanctified in Christ Jesus** (hēgiasmenois en Christō Iēsou - **ἡγιασμένοις ἐν Χριστῷ Ἰησοῦ), called to be saints..."**

Notice the phrasing. He does not write to "all religious people everywhere." He writes specifically to the **Ekklēsia tou Theou**—the Church of God. And who makes up this Church? Those who are **hēgiasmenois** (sanctified, set apart) **en Christō Iēsou** (in Christ Jesus).

This brings us to a vital, logical conclusion that connects directly to our previous chapter. We learned that to escape condemnation, you must be "in Christ." But how do you know you are truly "in Christ"? The Bible answers: by being part of His **Ekklēsia**, the body that He leads and sanctifies.

Christ did not establish thirty thousand conflicting denominations, each teaching a different gospel. The Apostle Paul was fiercely clear about this in **Ephesians 4:4-5**: **"There is one body** (hen sōma - **ἓν σῶμα) and one Spirit... one Lord, one faith, one baptism."**

One body. One faith. One truth.

To make this profoundly clear, let us use an analogy that a twelve-year-old can easily grasp, yet holds deep intellectual weight for the wisest scholar.

Imagine a ship navigating through a vast, violent, and pitch-black ocean during a terrible storm. The ocean represents the world, filled with crashing waves of false doctrines, confusing traditions, and deceptive spirits.

Out in the storm, the sailors might see faint, flickering lights dancing over the water. These are "will-o'-the-wisps"—natural phenomena that mimic light but lead ships directly into the rocks to be destroyed.

But on the shore, there is a massive, brilliant Lighthouse. This Lighthouse is built on a solid, unmovable rock foundation (the **Hedraiōma**). Its towering structure (the **Stylos**) holds a powerful, unwavering beam of light that cuts through the darkness, showing the **only** safe path into the harbor.

The Lighthouse does not say, **"Follow any light you like."** The Lighthouse says, **"Follow my light, for I am built on the rock, and I will bring you home safely."**

The true Church of God is that Lighthouse. It is not perfect because the humans inside it are perfect; it is true because the **foundation** it stands upon is the unadulterated Word of God, and the **light** it shines is the Gospel of Jesus Christ.

Why is this truth so emotionally resonant and practically valuable for you today?

Because it liberates you from the exhausting, paralyzing burden of having to figure out spiritual truth all by yourself. You do not have to guess what God wants. You do not have to be tossed to and fro by every new spiritual trend or viral theological opinion (Ephesians 4:14).

When you align yourself with the biblical **Ekklēsia**—the assembly that faithfully preaches the whole counsel of God, practices biblical baptism, keeps His commandments, and points solely to the resurrected Christ—you are stepping out of the stormy ocean of confusion and onto the solid rock of divine certainty.

This is not about religious pride or exclusivity for the sake of arrogance. It is about the profound, protective love of a Father who would never give His children a faulty map through a minefield. He gave us one true map. He built one true pillar.

To be "in Christ" is to be aligned with the teachings, practices, and identity of His true Church. It is to submit your heart to the **Stylos** and **Hedraiōma** of His truth.

As we turn the page, we will explore the practical, biblical markers of this true Church. How do you know you have found the right assembly? We will listen to the Master's own words: **"Where I am, there My servant will be also."**

Chapter 15: Where I Am, There My Servant Will Be Also

- **Description:** Based on **John 12:26** and **Hebrews 3:6**. A practical guide to identifying the true Church. It is not about grand buildings or human popularity, but about faithfulness to the Word of God, the keeping of His commandments (1 John 5:3), and the proclamation of the unadulterated Gospel of the Kingdom.

My beloved child, let us reason together.

We live in an age of overwhelming spiritual noise. If you drive down any major highway or scroll through any social media feed, you will see thousands of signs, logos, and advertisements for churches. Some promise prosperity, others promise emotional healing, and others promise spectacular entertainment. We are tempted to measure the truth of a church by its size, its wealth, its famous leaders, or the quality of its music.

But we must pause. We must apply clear, critical, and uncompromising logic. Since when does God measure truth by popularity? Since when does the Creator of the universe base His kingdom on human marketing?

We must ask the most sensible, grounding question a truth-seeker can ask: **"Ano ang sabi ng Biblia?"** (What does the Bible actually say about how to identify the true Church?)

The Master Teacher, our Lord Jesus Christ, did not leave us guessing. He gave us a precise, unadulterated, and logical formula to identify His true assembly. It has nothing to do with grand buildings, golden steeples, or viral fame. It has everything to do with alignment with His Word.

Listen to the definitive standard set by Christ Himself in **John 12:26**:

"If anyone serves Me, let him follow Me; and where I am, there My servant will be also."

Let us examine the original Greek text with the precision of a scholar and the clarity of a child. The word used for "serves" or "servant" is **Diakonos** (διάκονος). It means a waiter, an attendant, or one who executes the commands of another.

Notice the logical sequence Jesus establishes: First, you must **follow** Him. Second, because you follow Him, you will be **where He is**.

Jesus is not talking about a physical location on a map. He is talking about spiritual alignment. You cannot claim to be a **Diakonos** (servant) of Christ if you are walking in the opposite direction of His teachings. If Christ is in the truth, His true servants will be found in the truth. If Christ is humble, His true servants will be humble. Where the Master's teachings are faithfully upheld, there His true servants will be found.

The Apostle Paul reinforces this exact concept of divine ownership and governance in **Hebrews 3:6**:

"But Christ as a Son over His own house (oikos - **οἶκος**)**, whose house we are if we hold fast the confidence and the rejoicing of the hope firm to the end."**

The Greek word **Oikos** means a house, a household, or a family estate. Christ is not merely a guest in the church; He is the Son who has absolute authority **over His own house**.

But notice the crucial condition: **"whose house we are if we hold fast."** The Greek phrase for "hold fast" is **Kataschōmen** (κατάσχωμεν), which means to hold firmly, to retain, or to keep a tight grip on something. We are part of His household only if we firmly grip the truth He delivered, without letting go to grasp the shifting traditions of men.

How do we know if we are holding fast? How do we practically identify this true household in a world full of counterfeits? The Apostle John gives us the ultimate, measurable test in **1 John 5:3**:

"For this is the love of God, that we keep His commandments (entolai - **ἐντολαί). And His commandments are not burdensome."**

The Greek word **Entolai** refers to divine orders, precepts, or laws. The world defines love as a vague, warm feeling that demands nothing. But the Bible defines the love of God as measurable, active obedience.

If a group claims to be the Church of God, but they casually discard the commandments of God to accommodate modern culture, they are not holding fast. They are not following the Master. But where you find a people who reverently study the unadulterated Word of God, who practice biblical baptism, who reject the myths of the immortal soul, and who strive to keep the **Entolai** of the Creator out of genuine love—that is where you will find the true **Oikos**, the household of God.

To make this profoundly clear, let us use an analogy that a twelve-year-old can easily grasp, yet holds deep intellectual weight for the wisest scholar.

Imagine you are looking for the official, authentic workshop of a world-renowned Master Architect. You are lost in a massive, confusing city.

You see a building with bright neon lights, loud music, and a crowd of people cheering. But when you look inside, the workers are ignoring the Master's blueprints. They are building walls without foundations and using cheap, fragile materials. That is not the Master's workshop; it is a noisy imitation.

Then, you find another building. It might not have neon lights. It might be quiet. But when you look inside, you see the workers carefully studying the Master's original, signed blueprints. They are measuring twice. They are building exactly according to his design. And above the door, you see the Master's official seal.

How do you know you have found the true workshop? Not by the noise outside, but by the faithfulness to the blueprints inside.

The Bible is the Master's blueprint. The true Church is the workshop where those blueprints are followed exactly, without addition or subtraction.

Why is this truth so emotionally resonant and practically valuable for you today?

Because it liberates you from the deception of spiritual celebrity culture. You do not need to be dazzled by a charismatic speaker, a massive budget, or a trendy worship band to know you are in the presence of God's truth. Those things can be faked. Demons can mimic lights and sounds.

Instead, you are given a simple, unshakable test: **Are they following the Master's blueprints?**

Do they teach that the dead are asleep, as the Bible clearly states, or do they preach the myth of conscious ghosts? Do they point you to the grace and commandments of Christ, or do they point you to human traditions? Do they hold fast to the **Kataschōmen**, the firm grip on the hope of the resurrection?

If the answer is yes, you have found the **Oikos**. You have found the place where the Master is. And as He promised, **"Where I am, there My servant will be also."**

Do not be afraid to walk away from the noisy imitations. Step into the quiet, faithful, and powerful truth of God's true assembly. For it is only in His house, built on His foundation, holding fast to His Word, that you will find the genuine peace, the true identity, and the eternal life your soul was created to enjoy.

As we turn the page, we will leave behind the confusion of the world and step fully into the radiant, unshakable light of eternity. We will discover how this profound biblical truth destroys the fear of death forever, allowing us to live with a sound mind, a joyful heart, and a blessed hope.

PART VI: LIVING IN THE LIGHT OF ETERNITY

(Practical Value and Emotional Resonance for Daily Living)

Chapter 16: Freedom from the Fear of Death

- **Description:** A pastoral, healing chapter based on **Hebrews 2:14-15**. Jesus came to destroy the one who holds the power of death (the devil) and free those who were held in slavery by their fear of death. Readers are given practical, biblical tools to overcome anxiety, occult fears, and grief.

My beloved child, let us reason together.

There is a shadow that has haunted humanity since the dawn of time. It is the primal, universal ache that wakes us in the quiet hours of the night. It is the trembling we feel when a doctor delivers a grim diagnosis, the heavy silence at a graveside, and the deep, existential dread that whispers: **What happens when the light goes out?**

For centuries, this shadow has been weaponized. Religious systems, occult traditions, and human philosophies have used the terror of the unknown to control minds, extract wealth, and bind hearts in chains of anxiety. We have been taught to fear the dark, to dread the judgment of a vindictive deity, and to tremble at the thought of eternal, conscious torment.

But we must not live as captives to human myths. We must apply clear, critical, and compassionate logic. We must ask the most sensible, liberating question a truth-seeker can ask: **"Ano ang sabi ng Biblia?"** (What does the Bible actually say about our fear?)

The Apostle Paul, inspired by the Holy Spirit, delivers the most profound, healing diagnosis of the human condition in all of Scripture. Listen to the majestic, triumphant declaration in **Hebrews 2:14-15**:

"Inasmuch then as the children have partaken of flesh and blood, He Himself likewise shared in the same, that through death He might destroy (**katargēsē** - καταργήσῃ) the one who has the power of death, that is, the devil, and release (**apallaxē** - ἀπαλλάξῃ) those who through fear of death were subject to lifelong slavery (**doulia** - δουλεία)."

Let us examine this masterpiece of divine logic with the precision of a scholar and the heart of a child.

First, notice the enemy's weapon: **Phobos** (φόβος), meaning terror, dread, or panic. The enemy does not primarily use physical chains to keep humanity in bondage; he uses the **fear** of death.

Second, notice the enemy's title: **Diabolos** (διάβολος). This Greek word literally means "the slanderer" or "the false accuser." How does he slander God? By painting the Creator as a cruel torturer who keeps conscious souls burning forever, or by promoting the myth of wandering, suffering ghosts.

Third, notice the result of this deception: **Doulia** (δουλεία), meaning slavery, bondage, or lifelong servitude. Because people are terrified of what happens after death, they spend their entire lives serving false gods, consulting mediums, or living in paralyzing anxiety.

But then, notice the Master's glorious intervention. Jesus Christ, the Son of God, partook of flesh and blood. He did not avoid **Thanatos** (θάνατος - death). He walked straight into it. And why? **Hina katargēsē** (ἵνα καταργήσῃ) — "that He might destroy."

The Greek word **Katargeō** does not mean to annihilate the devil's physical existence right then and there. It means to render inoperative, to nullify, to strip of power, or to make a threat completely empty. Jesus did not just defeat death; He exposed the devil's ultimate threat as a bluff. He stripped the tyrant of his power.

To make this profoundly clear, let us use an analogy that a twelve-year-old can easily grasp, yet holds deep intellectual weight for the wisest scholar.

Imagine a cruel warden who guards a vast, dark prison. He tells the trembling prisoners, "If you ever try to leave this cell, the monstrous dragon waiting outside the door will devour your soul and torture you forever!"

Because the prisoners believe this lie, they are terrified. They obey the warden's every cruel command. They live in **Doulia** (lifelong slavery), bound not by iron bars, but by the **Phobos** (fear) of the dragon.

But one day, the King's own Son walks into the prison. He does not sneak out the back. He walks straight to the main door, opens it, and steps out to face the "dragon." And what does He find? He reveals that the dragon is nothing but a painted shadow on the wall, a trick of the warden's lantern. The King's Son shatters the lantern. The shadow vanishes.

Instantly, the warden's power is **Katargeō**—rendered completely inoperative. The threat is nullified. The prisoners are not physically dragged out; they are **Apallaxē**—released, freed, and invited to walk out the open door, realizing the monster was never real.

This is the breathtaking reality of the Gospel. The devil's greatest weapon was the lie that death leads to eternal, conscious torment or ghostly wandering. But Jesus passed through the grave, slept in the dust, and rose victorious. He proved that death is merely a sleep, and the grave is a temporary resting place under His sovereign control. The "dragon" of eternal conscious torment is a painted shadow of human tradition. The threat is nullified. The chains of fear are broken.

How, then, do we practically apply this liberating truth to overcome anxiety, occult fears, and grief in our daily lives? The Bible gives us three powerful, actionable tools.

Tool 1: Replace the Myth with the Map.

When the anxiety of death creeps in—whether for yourself or a loved one—do not let your imagination run wild with cultural myths. Actively replace the lie with the biblical map. Speak the truth aloud: **"My loved one is not suffering. They are not a wandering ghost. They are resting in the peaceful sleep of the Lord, as Ecclesiastes 9:5 and 1 Thessalonians 4:13 declare."** Truth is the antidote to terror.

Tool 2: Close the Door to the Occult.

You cannot claim to be free from the fear of death while simultaneously inviting deceiving spirits into your life. The Bible strictly forbids consulting the dead, using Ouija boards, or seeking out mediums (Deuteronomy 18:10-12). Why? Because these practices are the devil's counterfeit, designed to keep you in **Doulia** (bondage). When you feel the urge to seek a "sign" from the departed, firmly reject it. Declare: **"My loved one is asleep in Christ. I will not consult the dead, for I serve the God of the living."** Lock the door against the counterfeit, and peace will fill the room.

Tool 3: Anchor Your Heart in the Blessed Hope.

Grief is natural; despair is not. The Apostle Paul commands us in **1 Thessalonians 4:13** not to sorrow **"as others who have no hope."** When you weep, let your tears be watered by the **Elpis** (ἐλπίς - confident, joyful hope) of the resurrection. You are not saying a permanent goodbye. You are saying, **"Rest well, until the trumpet sounds."** This shifts your focus from the silent grave to the triumphant return of the King.

My beloved child, you were not created to live in the shadows. The Great Teacher did not endure the cross to leave you trembling in the dark. He shattered the tyrant's bluff. He holds the keys of Death and Hades (Revelation 1:18).

You are free. The monster is a shadow. The grave is a sleeping place. And the dawn of the resurrection is coming.

Lay down your heavy burden of fear. Breathe in the liberating air of God's truth. Walk out of the prison of anxiety, and step into the glorious, unshakable light of the Master's love.

As we turn the page, we will explore how this profound freedom transforms the way we comfort those who mourn, turning our deepest grief into a testament of unshakable, divine hope.

Chapter 17: Grieving with Hope

- **Description:** A tender, compassionate guide for the bereaved. Using **1 Thessalonians 4:13**, it teaches believers how to mourn without the despair of those who have no hope. We do not talk to the dead, but we talk to the God of the living about the dead, trusting in the promise of the morning resurrection.

My beloved child, let us reason together with a heart full of compassion and a mind anchored in truth.

There is no ache in the human experience quite like the silence left behind by a departed loved one. It is the empty chair at the dinner table. It is the unread text message on a glowing screen. It is the profound, echoing quiet of a room that once held their laughter. When death touches our lives, the heart naturally fractures, and tears flow. This is not a sign of weak faith; tears are the holy, natural language of love. Even the Master Teacher, our Lord Jesus Christ, wept at the tomb of His friend Lazarus (John 11:35).

But while grief is natural, the **manner** in which we grieve is deeply shaped by what we believe about death.

In our modern age, humanity is desperately trying to hack grief. We see a cultural rise in "grief-tech," artificial intelligence voice-cloning of the deceased, and a surge in spiritualist practices promising to keep our loved ones "with us." People are taught to talk to the sky, to leave out offerings for wandering spirits, or to desperately seek "signs" from the other side.

But we must pause. We must apply clear, critical, and deeply compassionate logic. We must ask the most sensible, grounding question a truth-seeker can ask: **"Ano ang sabi ng Biblia?"** (What does the Bible actually say about how we should mourn?)

The Apostle Paul, writing to a church that was deeply grieving the loss of their fellow believers, gives us the most tender, yet logically profound instruction on mourning in all of Scripture. Listen to his words in **1 Thessalonians 4:13**:

"But I do not want you to be ignorant, brethren, concerning those who have fallen asleep, lest you sorrow as others who have no hope."

Let us examine the original Greek text with the precision of a scholar and the tenderness of a shepherd.

Paul uses the word **Lypēsthe** (λυπῆσθε), which means to be grieved, to feel heaviness, or to experience sorrow. Notice carefully: Paul does **not** say, "Do not grieve." He does not demand that we suppress our tears or pretend we are not in pain. Grief is permitted.

What he forbids is the **quality** of that grief. He says we must not sorrow **Kathōs kai hoi loipoi hoi mē echontes elpida** (καθὼς καὶ οἱ λοιποὶ οἱ μὴ ἔχοντες ἐλπίδα) — "as the rest who have no hope."

The Greek word for hope here is **Elpis** (ἐλπίς). In biblical Greek, **Elpis** does not mean a vague, wishful thinking like, "I hope it doesn't rain tomorrow." It means a confident, joyful, and absolute expectation based on a sure promise.

Why can the believer grieve with **Elpis**, while the world grieves with absolute despair? Because we know the truth we have uncovered in this book: our loved ones have not vanished into a terrifying void, nor are they wandering as conscious, suffering ghosts. They have **Koimōmenous** (κοιμωμένους) — they have "fallen asleep."

To make this profoundly clear, let us use an analogy that a twelve-year-old can easily grasp, yet holds deep intellectual weight for the wisest scholar.

Imagine your dearest family member has to board a massive, beautiful ship for a long, necessary voyage across the ocean. The journey is peaceful, but while they are at sea, there is absolutely no cell phone signal. No internet. No way to call them.

Now, imagine standing on the dock, crying because you miss them. That is natural. But would you scream at the crashing waves, trying to talk to them? Would you hire a fraudulent "ocean medium" who claims they can channel messages from the ship, knowing full well the ship has no communication equipment? Would you live in terror, imagining your loved one is drowning or suffering in the dark hold of the ship?

Of course not. Why? Because you trust the Captain. You know the ship is safe. You know the voyage is temporary. You do not scream at the ocean; you simply wait at the dock, preparing your heart for the joyful morning when the ship returns and the gangway lowers.

This is the biblical reality of Christian grief.

When a loved one dies, they have boarded the ship of peaceful, dreamless sleep. The communication line of earthly consciousness is closed. Therefore, the most logical, biblical, and loving thing we can do is this: **We do not talk to the dead. We talk to the God of the living about the dead.**

When the ache of missing them is overwhelming, do not whisper into the empty air, hoping a ghost will hear you. Instead, fall on your knees and speak to the Father. Say, **"Lord, I miss them terribly. My heart is broken. But I thank You that they are no longer in pain. I thank You that they are resting safely in Your perfect memory. I trust You to keep them until the morning of the resurrection."**

This shift in focus is profoundly healing. It takes the heavy, superstitious burden off your shoulders and places it into the capable, loving hands of the Creator. It protects you from the manipulative traps of the occult, which prey on the vulnerable hearts of the grieving.

Furthermore, this truth redefines the cemetery. It is no longer a terrifying place of permanent loss. It is a sacred, quiet waiting room. It is the **Koimeterion** (κοιμητήριον), the sleeping place, where our loved ones rest free from the sickness, the tears, and the trials of this world.

The Apostle Paul continues in verse 14 to give us the ultimate foundation for our **Elpis** (hope):

"For if we believe that Jesus died and rose again, even so God will bring with Him those who sleep in Jesus."

Our hope is not anchored in the frailty of human memory or the deception of spiritualism. Our hope is anchored in the historical, undeniable fact of the Resurrection. Because Jesus conquered the grave, the grave is now merely a temporary cocoon.

So, my beloved child, if you are reading this with tears in your eyes, let them fall. Do not let anyone tell you that crying is a lack of faith. But let your tears be watered by the radiant light of biblical truth.

You are not grieving as those who have no hope. You are grieving as those who know the end of the story. You know that the silence of the grave is not an empty void; it is a sacred sanctuary guarded by the Almighty.

Hold fast to the **Elpis**. Wait at the dock. Trust the Captain. For the morning is coming, the trumpet will sound, and the sleepers will awake to a joy that will make all the tears of this world seem like a fleeting shadow.

As we turn the page, we will move from the comfort of grief to the urgency of action. We will explore the practical, vital steps you must take **today** to ensure that when that glorious morning arrives, you are numbered among those who will rise to everlasting life.

Chapter 18: The Final Choice

- **Description:** The powerful concluding call to action. Echoing **Deuteronomy 30:19** ("I have set before you life and death... therefore choose life"). A heartfelt invitation to surrender to Christ, be baptized into His true Church, and step out of the shadows of myth into the glorious, eternal light of biblical truth.

My beloved child, let us reason together one last time.

We have journeyed far. We have walked through the shadows of human tradition and emerged into the brilliant, liberating light of God's unadulterated Word. We have dismantled the terrifying myths of immortal ghosts, conscious torment, and spiritualist deception. We have uncovered the beautiful, peaceful reality that death is a dreamless sleep, and the grave is a sacred resting place under the sovereign care of the Creator. We have seen that the Master holds the keys to death and Hades, and that He will awaken His sleeping children in the twinkling of an eye.

But now, we arrive at the most critical moment of this entire journey. Knowledge alone is not enough. Understanding the truth does not automatically save you; it only gives you the map. You must now decide which path you will walk.

The Creator of the universe does not force His love or His truth upon anyone. He is a God of free will, and He places the ultimate decision squarely in your hands. Listen to the profound, loving invitation of the Almighty in **Deuteronomy 30:19**:

"I call heaven and earth as witnesses today against you, that I have set before you life and death, blessing and cursing; therefore choose life (**bacharta bachayim** - בָּחַרְתָּ בַּחַיִּים), that both you and your descendants may live."

Let us examine the original Hebrew with the precision of a scholar and the urgency of a shepherd. God declares that He has set before you **Chayim** (חַיִּים - life) and **Mavet** (מָוֶת - death). And then comes the divine imperative: **Bacharta** (בָּחַרְתָּ), which means "you shall choose."

God does not say, "I have forced life upon you." He says, "Choose." Why? Because love requires a choice. A forced relationship is not love; it is captivity. God desires willing servants, not programmed machines.

To make this profoundly clear, let us use an analogy that a twelve-year-old can easily grasp, yet holds deep intellectual weight for the wisest scholar.

Imagine you have spent your entire life sitting in a vast, dark, cold theater. On the stage, there are beautiful, glowing holograms of spirits and ghosts. They whisper comforting but false things to you. You have lived your whole life watching this play, afraid to leave your seat, believing the illusions are all that exist.

But then, the Great Director of the universe walks down the aisle. He takes your hand and points to a heavy, real, wooden door at the back of the theater. He says, **"The holograms are just light and deception. They cannot save you. But outside this door is the actual, warm, brilliant sunrise. You must choose to stand up, walk away from the illusions, and open the door."**

Choosing life is not just nodding your head at the Director's words. Choosing life is standing up, turning your back on the glowing illusions, and walking through that door into the real light.

How, then, do we practically, biblically, and definitively "choose life" today? The Scriptures give us four clear, actionable steps to step out of the shadows of myth and into the eternal light of biblical truth.

First: Repentance (Metanoia - μετάνοια)

You must make a decisive, complete change of mind. The Greek word **Metanoia** means to think differently afterward. It is not merely feeling sorry for your past mistakes. It is a radical, willful U-turn. It is looking at the myths of ghosts, the fear of death, and the traditions of men, and saying, **"I reject these lies. I turn my back on them, and I turn my face entirely toward the truth of God's Word."**

Second: Faith (Pistis - πίστις)

You must place your absolute, unwavering trust in the Resurrected Savior. As we learned, Jesus Christ alone holds the **Kleis** (κλεῖς - keys) of Death and Hades (Revelation 1:18). Faith is leaning your entire weight upon the promise that His sacrifice paid the penalty for your sins, and that His resurrection guarantees your own. It is trusting the Captain of your salvation completely.

Third: Baptism (Baptisma - βάπτισμα)

Faith must be acted upon. The Apostle Peter declares in **Acts 2:38**: **"Repent, and let every one of you be baptized in the name of Jesus Christ for the remission of sins."** The Greek word **Baptizō** (βαπτίζω) means to immerse or submerge completely. This is not a mere sprinkling of water; it is a profound, physical enactment of the Gospel. When you go under the water, you are burying the old, myth-bound, fearful self. When you rise from the water, you are publicly declaring that you are rising to walk in newness of life, united with Christ's resurrection (Romans 6:4-5). It is the moment you step through the wooden door into the sunrise.

Fourth: Alignment with the True Church (Ekklēsia - ἐκκλησία)

You cannot choose life in isolation. Christ did not leave His truth to be scattered among thousands of conflicting, man-made traditions. He established His **Ekklēsia**—the called-out assembly, the Church of

God—as the sole pillar and ground of the truth (1 Timothy 3:15). To choose life is to humbly submit your heart to the teachings, practices, and fellowship of the true body of believers who faithfully uphold the unadulterated Word of God, keep His commandments out of love, and eagerly await the blessed hope of His return.

My beloved child, the time for hesitation is over. The cultural noise is loud, and the enemy of your soul will try to whisper doubts, fears, and familiar illusions to pull you back into the dark theater. But you now possess the unshakable armor of biblical truth.

You know that your departed loved ones are not suffering; they are sleeping peacefully in the Master's care.

You know that you are not a ghost trapped in a machine, but a magnificent, unified creation, animated by the breath of the Almighty.

You know that the grave is not a permanent prison, but a temporary waiting room for the glorious morning of the resurrection.

The trumpet will sound. The archangel will shout. The sleeping **nephesh** will be clothed in incorruptible, immortal glory.

The only question that remains is this: When that glorious morning arrives, and the Master calls your name, will you be found resting securely in Him?

Do not let another day pass in the shadows of fear and myth. Stand up. Turn away from the illusions. Take the hand of the Savior. Repent, believe, be baptized, and join the faithful assembly of God.

Choose life. Choose the truth. Choose the glorious, eternal light that shines from the face of the Resurrected King.

"He who has an ear, let him hear what the Spirit says to the churches." (Revelation 2:7).

May the grace of our Lord Jesus Christ, the love of God the Father, and the comforting, guiding presence of the Holy Spirit be with you always, as you step boldly into the eternal dawn. Amen.

APPENDIX A: The Lexicon of Life and Death

To truly understand God's Word, we must listen to it in its original voice. Below is a clear, definitive guide to the foundational Hebrew and Greek words regarding life, death, and the afterlife, complete with their Strong's Concordance references and exact biblical definitions.

Hebrew (Old Testament)

1. **Nephesh** (נֶפֶשׁ) | **Strong's H5315**

Definition: A breathing creature, a living being, life, or person.

Biblical Truth: It is not an immortal ghost. Humans and animals are both described as **nephesh**. Man **became** a living **nephesh** (Genesis 2:7); he was not given one. The **nephesh** that sins, it shall die (Ezekiel 18:4).

2. **Ruach** (רוּחַ) | **Strong's H7307**

Definition: Breath, wind, or the animating spirit/power of life given by God.

Biblical Truth: It is the divine energy that sustains life. When a person dies, the **ruach** (breath of life) returns to God who gave it, and the person returns to dust (Ecclesiastes 12:7). It is not a conscious, floating personality.

3. **Sheol** (שְׁאוֹל) | **Strong's H7585**

Definition: The grave, the pit, or the state of death.

Biblical Truth: It is the common destination of all humanity. It is a place of silence and unconscious sleep (**Dumah**), not a place of conscious torment or ghostly activity (Psalm 115:17; Ecclesiastes 9:10).

Greek (New Testament)

4. **Psyche** (ψυχή) | **Strong's G5590**

Definition: The New Testament equivalent of **nephesh**; a living being, life, or person.

Biblical Truth: It refers to the whole person. The Bible explicitly states that a **psyche** can die (Revelation 16:3) and must be saved from death (James 5:20), proving it is mortal, not inherently immortal.

5. **Pneuma** (πνεῦμα) | **Strong's G4151**

Definition: Breath, wind, or spirit.

Biblical Truth: Just as **ruach** animates the body, **pneuma** is the breath of life. A body without **pneuma** is dead (James 2:26).

6. **Hades** (ᾅδης) | **Strong's G86**

Definition: The grave or the state of death; the New Testament equivalent of **Sheol**.

Biblical Truth: It is not the mythological underworld of torture. It is the holding place of the dead, from which Christ holds the keys (Revelation 1:18), awaiting the resurrection.

7. **Koimao** (κοιμάω) | **Strong's G2837**

Definition: To fall asleep, to slumber.

Biblical Truth: The consistent biblical metaphor for death. It denotes a temporary, unconscious state of rest from which one will be awakened by Christ (John 11:11; 1 Thessalonians 4:13).

8. **Anastasis** (ἀνάστασις) | **Strong's G386**

Definition: A standing up again; resurrection.

Biblical Truth: The glorious, instantaneous event where the sleeping dead are raised and clothed in immortality by the power of Christ (1 Corinthians 15:52).

APPENDIX B: The "What About...?" Apologetics Guide

When you share this truth, you will encounter objections rooted in tradition. Do not be shaken. Let the Bible interpret the Bible. Here are direct, verse-by-step answers to the most common challenges.

1. "What about the Witch of Endor summoning Samuel?" (1 Samuel 28)

The Objection: If the dead are asleep, how could the witch of Endor bring up the prophet Samuel to speak to King Saul?

The Biblical Answer: The Bible explicitly states that God had already rejected Saul for his disobedience and had stopped answering him by any means (1 Samuel 28:6). God does not break His own divine law (Deuteronomy 18:10-12) to answer a witch. Furthermore, the entity that appeared said to Saul, **"Why have you disturbed me?"** (1 Samuel 28:15). If Samuel were resting peacefully in the presence of God, he would not be "disturbed" or dragged back to earth by a pagan ritual. This was a demonic deception—a familiar spirit (**Ov**) mimicking Samuel's appearance and knowledge to deliver a final, condemning message to a rebellious king. God permitted the deception as judgment, but it was not the actual, conscious soul of Samuel.

2. "What about being 'absent from the body, present with the Lord'?" (2 Corinthians 5:8)

The Objection: Doesn't this verse prove that the moment we die, our spirit goes straight to heaven?

The Biblical Answer: We must never isolate a single phrase from its context. In 2 Corinthians 5:1-4, Paul contrasts our current earthly body (a "tent") with our future resurrection body (a "building from God"). Paul expresses a deep desire to be **"clothed"** with this resurrection body. He explicitly states in verse 4: **"Not that we would be unclothed, but further clothed, that mortality may be swallowed up by life."**

To be "unclothed" is to be dead and asleep in the grave. Paul's longing to be "present with the Lord" is not a desire for the intermediate state of death (sleep), but a passionate longing for the **resurrection**, when we will be fully "clothed" in immortality and stand face-to-face with Christ. The "presence" is achieved **through** the resurrection, not at the moment of death.

3. "What about Elijah being taken up to heaven?" (2 Kings 2:11)

The Objection: Elijah didn't die; a chariot of fire took him to heaven, proving some people bypass death and the grave.

The Biblical Answer: The Hebrew word used for "heaven" in 2 Kings 2:11 is **Shamayim** (שָׁמַיִם). This word has three biblical meanings: the atmospheric sky (where birds fly, Genesis 1:20), outer space (stars), and the dwelling place of God. Elijah was taken up into the **atmospheric sky (shamayim)**, just as the whirlwind lifted him.

How do we know he did not go to God's eternal dwelling? Because years later, Elijah was still on earth and wrote a letter to King Jehoram of Judah (2 Chronicles 21:12). Furthermore, the New Testament confirms that the faithful prophets of old, including Elijah, **"died in faith, not having received the promises"** but are waiting for the resurrection (Hebrews 11:13, 39-40). Elijah slept, and he awaits the glorious morning of the resurrection like all the faithful.

APPENDIX C: The Pathway to the True Church

You have learned that being "in Christ" is the only hope for the resurrection of life. But how do you find the assembly that faithfully represents Him? Do not be swayed by grand buildings, emotional manipulation, or human popularity. Use this biblical checklist to find the true **Ekklēsia** (ἐκκλησία):

1. **They Submit to the Supreme Authority of Scripture.**

Do they say, **"To the law and to the testimony! If they do not speak according to this word, it is because there is no light in them"** (Isaiah 8:20)? The true church does not elevate human tradition, creeds, or feelings above the plain, unadulterated Word of God.

2. **They Teach the Whole Counsel of God.**

Do they faithfully teach the biblical reality of the mortal soul, the unconscious sleep of the dead, and the literal, physical resurrection? Or do they preach the comforting but unbiblical myths of immortal ghosts and eternal conscious torment? The true church guards the **Stylos** and **Hedraiōma** (pillar and foundation) of truth (1 Timothy 3:15).

3. **They Practice Biblical Baptism.**

Do they baptize by full immersion (**baptizō**) in the name of Jesus Christ, teaching that it is the biblical moment of remission of sins and union with Christ's death and resurrection (Acts 2:38; Romans 6:4)? The true church does not reduce this sacred command to a mere symbolic sprinkle.

4. **They Keep the Commandments of God.**

Jesus said, **"If you love Me, keep My commandments"** (John 14:15). The true church teaches that grace does not abolish God's law; rather, it empowers believers to obey it out of genuine love (1 John 5:3; Revelation 14:12).

5. **They Proclaim the Blessed Hope.**

Do they eagerly await the visible, triumphant return of Jesus Christ and the resurrection of the dead? The true church lives with its eyes on the horizon, comforting one another with the promise of the trumpet and the awakening of the **nephesh** (1 Thessalonians 4:18).

If you find an assembly that faithfully aligns with these biblical markers, you have found the household of God. Step inside, and step into the truth.

We Cordially Invite You To Study and Joined the Doctrines of Jesus Christ through the
Members Church Of God International
https://mcgi.org
https://mcgi.org/mass-indoctrination/#lang-tl

With heartfelt thanks for your support,

—JV SETH

Hard Life Problems Worth Solving

is a series that confronts the deepest struggles we face—not with quick fixes, but with clarity, courage, and lasting wisdom.

Please Visit, Read, Rate My Books and Follow

https://www.amazon.com/author/jvseth

BACK COVER BLURB

Are you tired of living in fear of the dark, haunted by myths of wandering spirits and eternal torment?

For centuries, humanity has been held captive by a terrifying lie: the belief that death is a conscious, ghostly wandering or a gateway to unending suffering. This myth has left millions paralyzed by grief, vulnerable to occult deception, and deeply confused about the Creator's true character.

But what if everything you've been taught about the afterlife is wrong?

In **SOUL SLEEP: The Shocking Biblical Truth That Shatters Ghost Myths and Reveals God's Amazing Plan for the Dead**, you will embark on a profound, life-changing journey back to the unadulterated, original text of Scripture. Written with the compassionate heart of a shepherd and the razor-sharp logic of a master Bible scholar, this book dismantles human tradition and replaces it with the glorious, liberating truth of God's Word.

Drawing exclusively from the original Hebrew and Greek texts, this masterpiece provides the ultimate **apologetics against spiritualism and mediums**, exposing the dangerous deceptions of the modern occult. You will discover that the dead do not haunt us, nor do they suffer. Instead, they rest in a profound, dreamless slumber, safely preserved in the memory of the Almighty.

Inside this groundbreaking book, you will discover:

- **The Original Hebrew and Greek Bible Meanings:** Uncover the true definitions of **nephesh** (soul), **ruach** (spirit), and

sheol (the grave), proving once and for all that the soul is mortal and death is a sleep.
- **Comforting Scripture for Loss of a Loved One:** Replace the agony of hopeless grief with the "blessed hope" of the resurrection, learning how to mourn with peace and divine assurance.
- **The True State of the Dead Bible Study:** A clear, logical, and deeply scholarly examination of why the grave is silent, and why God strictly forbids consulting the departed.
- **The Resurrection of the Righteous and the Wicked:** A breathtaking, verse-by-verse look at the "twinkling of an eye" awakening, and the biblical reality of the "second death" as complete destruction, not eternal conscious torment.
- **Practical Wisdom for Overcoming Fear of Dying and the Occult:** Actionable, biblical tools to break free from superstitious anxiety and step into the unshakable freedom of Christ.

This is not just a book; it is a spiritual liberation. It is the definitive guide for anyone seeking **conditional immortality and annihilationism** explained with clarity, grace, and absolute biblical fidelity.

Stop letting human myths dictate your eternal hope. It is time to lay down the heavy burden of fear and embrace the radiant, comforting light of biblical truth.

"Read It," and discover the peace that only the unadulterated Word of God can provide.

BACK COVER BLURB

(Designed for the physical paperback and hardcover. Read time: ~35 seconds.)

Are the dead really watching us from the shadows?

For generations, we have been taught to fear the grave, believing that our loved ones become wandering, conscious spirits. But this comforting myth has birthed a terrifying reality: spiritual confusion, occult deception, and hopeless grief.

It is time to ask the most important question of all: **What does the Bible actually say?**

In **SOUL SLEEP**, master Bible scholarship meets profound pastoral compassion. Stripping away centuries of human tradition, this book reveals the breathtaking, original Hebrew and Greek truth: **Death is not a haunting; it is a holy sleep.**

Discover why the grave is utterly silent, how to find genuine comfort in the loss of a loved one, and why the resurrection of Jesus Christ is the only true key to eternal life.

Lay down your fear. Embrace the truth. The morning of the resurrection is coming.

"You will know the truth, and the truth will set you free." — John 8:32

Made in the USA
Coppell, TX
05 November 2026

11286711R00068